The Peak District

C000140441

Andrew McCloy

Edited by Ian Johnson

*An independent guide to over 200 pubs
in and around the Peak District*

Johnson Publishing

Published by:
Johnson Publishing
160 Sutton Road, Mansfield
Nottinghamshire NG18 5HH
email: johnson.publishing@virgin.net

First Edition 2002
Reprinted 2003

Cover: The Bull's Head, Monyash, Derbyshire
Back Cover: Doorway of The Red Lion, Litton, Derbyshire

Acknowledgements:
Thanks to Penny Edmonds, Cliff Rowbotham, and Neil Summers for their invaluable
help in researching this guide, and to numerous landlords and landladies for their
cooperation and assistance.

ISBN 0-9542574-0-5

Printed by The Reliance Press Ltd, Mansfield, Nottinghamshire

CONTENTS

Map showing areas included in this guide

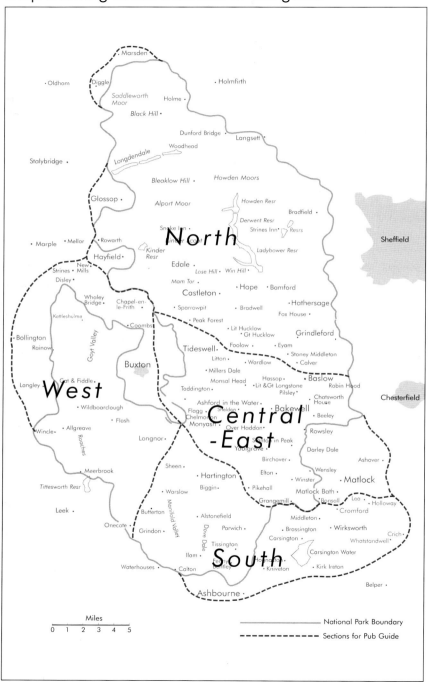

- Marsden
- Oldham
- Diggle
- Holmfirth
Saddleworth Moor
- Holme
Black Hill
- Dunford Bridge
- Langsett
- Woodhead
- Stalybridge
Longdendale
- Bleaklow Hill
- Howden Moors
- Glossop
- Alport Moor
- Howden Resr
- Bradfield
Derwent Resr
- Strines Inn
- Resrs
- Marple
- Mellor
- Rowarth
North
Kinder Resr
- Ladybower Resr
- Sheffield
- Hayfield
New Mills
- Strines
- Disley
- Edale
Lose Hill · Win Hill ·
Mam Tor ·
- Castleton
- Hope
- Bamford
- Whaley Bridge
Chapel-en-le-Frith
- Sparrowpit
- Bradwell
- Hathersage
Fox House ·
- Kettleshulme
- Coombs
- Peak Forest
- Lit Hucklow
- Gt Hucklow
- Grindleford
- Bollington
- Rainow
Goyt Valley
- Tideswell
- Foolow
- Eyam
- Stoney Middleton
Litton ·
- Wardlow
- Calver
- Buxton
- Millers Dale
- Langley
West
Cat & Fiddle
Monsal Head
- Hassop
- Baslow
- Wincle
- Allgreave
Roaches
- Taddington
- Lit &Gt Longstone
- Robin Hood
Pilsley ·
- Chatsworth House
- Chesterfield
- Wildboarclough
- Ashford in the Water
- Flagg
- Sheldon
- Bakewell
- Beeley
- Flash
- Chelmorton
- Monyash
Central -East
- Over Haddon
- Rowsley
- Meerbrook
- Longnor
- Youlgrave
- Birchover
- Darley Dale
- Ashover
- Sheen
- Hartington
- Elton
- Wensley
- Tittesworth Resr
- Warslow
- Biggin
- Pikehall
- Winster
Matlock
- Matlock Bath
- Leek
- Grangemill
- Bonsall
- Lea
- Holloway
- Butterton
- Alstonefield
- Middleton
- Cromford
- Onecote
- Grindon
- Parwich
- Brassington
- Wirksworth
Manifold Valley
- Carsington
- Whatstandwell
- Crich
Dove Dale
- Tissington
South
- Carsington Water
- Ilam
- Kniveton
- Kirk Ireton
- Waterhouses
- Calton
- Belper
- Ashbourne

```
Miles
0   1   2   3   4   5
```

──────── National Park Boundary

- - - - - - - - Sections for Pub Guide

4

INTRODUCTION

Welcome to the first-ever guide to the pubs and inns of the Peak District. Did you know, incidentally, that there are over 50,000 pubs throughout Great Britain? Roughly-speaking this works out as one for every 1000 people, and the good news is that a fair few of them are to be found in the Peak District, a delightful area of undulating dales and high purple moorland sandwiched between Manchester, Sheffield and the East Midlands. The core of this important recreational zone is the Peak National Park, founded in 1951 as Britain's first, and still by far the most popular National Park in the country. However, this guidebook goes beyond the administrators' boundaries and embraces many of the fascinating old Peakland towns that encircle the National Park: Matlock, Buxton, Ashbourne, Wirksworth and Glossop are all included, as well as a vast swathe of the rolling green countryside in the south-east of the region that is still essential Peak District.

In the following pages you will find details of over 200 establishments, from tranquil village inns to busy town centre bars, historic roadside taverns to modern, family-oriented pubs. They cover six separate counties or authorities: Derbyshire, Staffordshire, Cheshire, Greater Manchester, South Yorkshire and West Yorkshire. However, it's important to state the rather obvious fact that not every public house in the Peak District has been included. During our research we have been careful to inspect and judge every pub on its individual merit, and inevitably there were some that for one reason or another didn't make the grade. With the larger centres, in particular, we have tried to present a cross-section of the more original and interesting pubs, and not necessarily the biggest or grandest, nor for that matter always the most popular in terms of sheer numbers of customers.

Another obvious point that still needs stating is that while we have made every effort at accuracy the information that follows is subject to change, often unannounced and sudden - from closures of breweries (affecting tied pubs) and national chains selling their properties, through to the sudden departure of a chef or a landlord taken ill. The publisher cannot be held responsible for any errors or omissions and if you have comments or suggestions about pubs included (or possibly not yet featured), please send them to the address at the front of this book.

Peak pubs by area:

For the purposes of the guide the Peak District has been divided into four areas, the largest of which is the **Central/Eastern** Area. For many new visitors to the National Park this is often the core area, since it encompasses much of the Wye and Derwent valleys, Chatsworth House and Haddon Hall, the 'resort' of Matlock Bath, plus the popular towns of Bakewell and Matlock. And apart from these last two centres the area is dominated by a whole host of attractive villages that are scattered across the rolling dales and upland plateau. There are pockets of gritstone moor, principally along the eastern edge of the Derwent Valley, but above all this is a typical White Peak landscape, so-called because of the pearly-white limestone that is evident not just in the walls and buildings but also poking out of some of the thinly-grassed fields and dales. The Central/Eastern Area is the place for a leisurely riverside ramble or a stroll through the meadows, followed by an unhurried lunch in a peaceful village pub. Places like Beeley, Over Haddon, Miller's Dale, Monyash and Youlgrave all come to mind.

The **Northern** Area is markedly different, for here we travel into the Dark Peak where the limestone gives way to millstone grit, and is typified by the bleak upland moors and bogs of Kinder Scout, Bleaklow and Black Hill. It's a rugged, wild landscape, punctured by the reservoirs of the Upper Derwent Valley, where the rock face of Stanage Edge and the windy hilltop miles of the Pennine Way provide some challenging outdoor pursuits. And yet this glorious open landscape is all within easy reach of Sheffield and Manchester. There's interest underground with the show caverns of Castleton, while you can take to the air with the gliders at Great Hucklow. As far as the spread of pubs is concerned they tend to get sparser as the South Pennines of Yorkshire draw near, but often their isolated setting is part of the appeal. The Strines Inn, Snake Pass Inn, Ladybower Inn and Stanhope Arms Inn at Dunford Bridge are all good examples.

Gritstone moorland is also a feature of the **Western** Area, with a high upland barrier running south along the Derbyshire/Cheshire border. Small urban pockets exist around New Mills, Chapel-en-le-Frith and Whaley Bridge, and of course there's the busy regional centre of Buxton with its spa heritage. Elsewhere, though, it's mostly empty green hills and secretive valleys, such as the Upper Goyt, offering some great walking and fine views. It's a wilder and less harnessed landscape than the limestone dales of the Central/East, but the scattering of hidden villages and hamlets still reveal a store of delightful pubs that are often well off the main tourist track - try Wildboarclough, Langley, Wincle, Meerbrook and Longnor.

The **Southern** Area is typified by rather more gentle scenery, for once we move away from the Staffordshire Moorlands in the far west we're back amid the undulating dales of limestone country. Highlights include the deep cleft of the Manifold Valley and spectacular Dove Dale, with its caves, sheer rock faces and famous stepping stones. Wirksworth and Ashbourne are popular market towns, and from near the latter the Tissington Trail cycle route heads off to join the High Peak Trail north of Hartington. There's also plenty to see and do at Carsington Water, while the wooded hillsides around Lea and Cromford provide some quiet and scenic walking. For a decent pint and a tasty home-made meal visit the likes of Alderwasley, Butterton, Alstonefield, Brassington and Warslow.

How to use this guide – sample entry:

The Peak District Inn

Much Boozing, Derbyshire. (01234) 567891
Grid ref: 765432
Open 12-3, 7-11; 12-2, 7-10.30 Sun.
Beer: Imbibers Best Bitter, Old Hangover; Landlady's Revenge plus one guest beer such as Ploughman's Furrow.
Food: Wide range of hot and cold food, snacks and main meals, with specials such as spicy ostrich curry, and roast beetroot and dandelion casserole. Served 12-2, 7-9 daily in both bars or no-smoking dining room. Range of vegetarian choices, and children's menu.
Accommodation: B&B - 2 en-suite doubles and 1 twin room; campsite in adjoining field.
General: A delightful 17th century inn overlooking the village green, made up of two small bars with open fires and authentic beams, scrubbed pine furniture and original prints, plus a spacious no-smoking room. Briefly a Royalist base in the Civil War, the pub is supposedly haunted by a rowdy Cavalier who slams doors and sings bawdy songs in the cellar. Children welcome until 8.30pm, plus there's a large beer garden with swings and slides. Disabled toilet, and wheelchair ramp from car park at rear. Free folk sessions every Wed eve. Dogs allowed in tap room only.

OPENING HOURS: These can vary in slack periods, such as Mondays and Tuesdays, especially in the case of out-of-the-way country pubs. Other places operate different summer and winter opening times, and where known this is clearly stated, with the summer times being shown in brackets. A typical pub may have its opening times denoted in the following ways -

1) Open: 11-2, 7-11; 12-10.30 Sun.

The pub is open (all year) Monday to Saturday: 11am to 2pm and 7pm to 11pm. (Saturday opening times are only shown separately if they differ from the Monday to Friday times.) Sundays: from 12noon to 10.30pm.

2) Open: 11-2, 7-11 (11-11 summer); 12-10.30 Sun.

As 1) - but in summer it is open from 11am to 11pm Monday to Saturday. There are many and various permutations of opening times within the guide, and these have been presented in a (hopefully) logical and systematic method. An example of a pub with more complicated opening times would be: Open: 6-11 (12-3, 6-11 Mon-Fri summer); 12-3, 6-11 (11-11 summer) Sat; 12-3, 6-10.30 (12-10.30 summer) Sun.

Introduction

This means in winter opening times are; Mondays to Fridays 6pm to 11pm. Saturdays 12 noon to 3pm and 6pm to 11pm. Sundays 12 noon to 3pm and 6pm to 11 pm. In summer times are; Mondays to Fridays 12 noon to 3pm and 6pm to 11pm. Saturdays 11am to 11pm. Sundays 12noon to 10.30pm. So, that's all clear then? (No I havn't made this up, it's the Beehive at Combs.) N.B. If a landlord says he is open all day, this means all the currently permitted hours, which are 11am to 11pm Mondays to Saturdays and 12 noon to 10.30pm Sundays. There may be legislation over the next year or so which will allow more liberalised opening hours (this may or may not make life easier for pub guide compilers).

BEER: Only cask conditioned real ales (hand-pull beers) are cited. These are beers that are 'live', i.e there is still yeast in the cask, and the beer continues to mature and gain flavour in the cellar (as opposed to 'keg' beers, which are pasteurised and lack the subtle flavour and variety of real ales.) Like food choices off the specials board, the availability of real ales can vary from place to place. 'Guest' or 'seasonal' beers are just that - real ales that the landlord gets in from time to time - and those listed are the ones we found when we visited or those that had been on previously. There is no guarantee that they will be on when you visit. An example of a beer list might be -

Beer: Theakston's Best Bitter, Old Peculier; Whim Hartington Bitter, plus one guest beer such as Abbeydale Absolution.

Where a pub stocks more than one beer from the same brewery the subsequent beer follows a comma, without repeating the brewery name. In the above example the first two beers are Theakson's Best Bitter and Theakston's Old Peculier. An additional beer from a different brewery follows a semicolon. In this case the third beer is Hartington Bitter from the Whim Brewery. The guest beer in this example is Absolution from the Abbeydale Brewery. Where pubs offer an impressively varied or selective wine list, or other specialities such as a range of real coffees, unusual cider, malt whiskies, etc, they are mentioned, but of course we do not pretend to have tasted them all! Wine, for instance, is now served in just about every pub, but the quality can vary enormously. The top eating pubs generally have a decent list, but like any restaurant don't always count on it.

FOOD: It should go without saying, but the best places are always subject to availability of fresh produce, and menus can and do change seasonally. Serving hours may be reduced at quiet times. Special dishes quoted are examples of what we found when we visited, and of course there's no assurance that they'll be on at other dates. Some were sampled, but regretfully not all, and of course we have not eaten extensively in each pub. Inevitably pubs have busy periods, and the best eating places are often fully booked at weekends and on Bank Holidays - so ring ahead if you want to be sure of securing a table. Similarly, if you have a special diet make a call in advance to check whether they can cater for you, and speak to the manager or kitchen staff. Many pubs have children's menus, but the more enterprising serve half portions of main adult meals at half the price, so always enquire.

CHILDREN: We specifically asked each landlord whether they had any restrictions on adults with children (any age) from entering their pub, and also whether there was any dedicated play area inside or out. Always bear in mind that children, like adults, are admitted at the landlord's discretion - bad-behaviour in a public house is not tolerated from any age group.

WHEELCHAIR ACCESS: Although plenty of pubs in this guide are on pavement level or perhaps just have a couple of steps at the door, and regularly welcome wheelchair guests, we have only identified pubs where ramps, entrances and toilets have been specifically installed or adapted for people with disabilities.

DOGS: This is where pubs specifically allow well-behaved dogs inside, or in a few cases where a canine-loving landlord makes dogs especially welcome. Other pubs may allow dogs on the premises away from eating areas or after certain times, but it is always at their discretion, and you must check first.

LIVE MUSIC: Loosely defined by us as one or more people performing 'live' music on a regular basis (weekly or monthly) in a pub, usually free of charge and sometimes encouraging audience participation. It may vary from folk sessions to jazz evenings, a solo performer or duet, but does not include karaoke or a chap with a music box and flashing lights.

ACCOMMODATION: We have merely listed the type of accommodation provided by each establishment (bed and breakfast, self-catering, camping, etc) and where relevant the number of rooms, units, pitches, etc. No inspection of any kind has been made. You are strongly urged to ring ahead for any available brochure or visit the pub's web site for more details, and also check with the local tourist information centre for their graded listings.

Publisher's note: It is our policy that pubs appear in the guide on merit only; no payments have been received or sought by the author or publisher. All research visits were made 'incognito' and without prior notice. We only made ourselves known after purchasing food/drink.

Part One: Central / Eastern Area

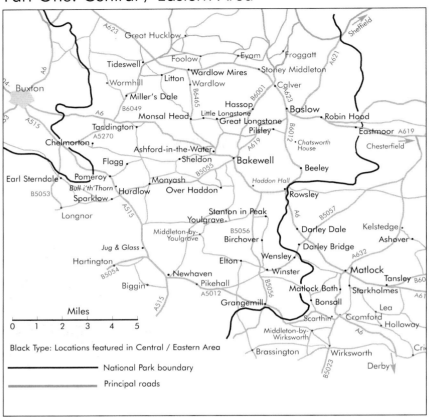

Black Type: Locations featured in Central / Eastern Area

━━━━━━━━━━━━━━━ National Park boundary

━━━━━━━━━━━━━━━ Principal roads

Ashford in the Water - Derbyshire

Sheepwash Bridge, Ashford in the Water

It's every visitor's idea of the perfect Peak District village: winding streets of neat and tidy stone cottages, a handsome medieval bridge, picturesque cricket ground, and so on. Unfortunatley that means summer weekends can be very busy, so choose your moment to admire Sheepwash Bridge (where animals are still occasionally dipped in the River Wye) and the parish church. Inside which are some examples of a local polished limestone known as Ashford Black Marble that was once mined at nearby Rookery Wood and Arrock Quarry. Well-dressing takes place in early June when six wells are ritually decorated. And in case you're wondering, the sandbags outside some cottage doors are testimony to the village's vulnerability to the Wye's regular flooding - when the village is sometimes referred to locally as Ashford under Water!

Access: 1½ miles north-west of Bakewell (off A6).

Ashford Arms Hotel

Church Street. Tel: (01629) 812725
Grid ref: 196697
Open: 11-11; 12-10.30 Sun.
Beer: Tetley Bitter; Bass or Stones, plus two guest beers.
Food: Lunchtime and evening, 'till 8.45. Extensive menu and range of bar snacks, plus full wine list. Separate dining room, and no-smoking bar and conservatory.
Accommodation: B&B - 9 en-suite rooms, two including 4-poster beds.
General: A plush, 18th century coaching inn, whose new owners are planning to introduce features such as a children's pet

corner in the large beer garden, plus a jazz evening for rather older customers. Large well decorated rooms, including a disabled toilet and tap room with pool table. Walkers welcome.

Bull's Head

Church Street. Tel (01629) 812931
Grid ref: 195696
Open: 11-3, 6-11; 12-3, 6-10.30 Sun.
Beer: Robinson's Best Bitter, Old Stockport Bitter plus Robinson's seasonal beer.
Food: Lunchtime and evening, 6.30-9. Mouthwatering specials board, includes Steak and Old Stockport Pie with braised cabbage, and venison and cranberry sausage with garlic mashed potatoes.
General: A comfortable, solid local, off the main street, with patio seating outside. Two bars, with open fire and gentle piped music, and plenty of seating. Children in family room only. Called the Turk's Head in the 1800's, it's been run by the same family since the 1950s.

ASHOVER - Derbyshire

Located on the eastern fringe of the region, 'Asher' is a rather strung-out but nevertheless attractive Peakland village that has its fair share of visitors - not least because this has been a location for the filming of TV's 'Peak Practice'. Perhaps of more lasting interest is the Church of All Saints, with its historic Norman font made out of local lead, and an impressive 16th century alabaster tomb of Thomas Babington and his wife.

Access: 3 miles north-east of Matlock (off A632).

Black Swan

Church Street. Tel (01246) 590305
Grid ref: 350636
Open: 11-3, 6-11; 11-11 Sat; 12-10.30 Sun.
Beer: Tetley Bitter; Bass, plus a guest beer (such as Timothy Taylor's Landlord; Charles Wells Bombardier).
Food: Lunchtime and evening menus served in bar or in the no-smoking dining room ('till 9pm each evening). Choice of sandwiches and cobs through to home-made hot dishes, including filled Large

11

Central / Eastern

Yorkshire Puddings, steaks and various fish dishes. Vegetarian and children's options always available.

General: Handsome 300 year old building, whose one long bar originally housed an undertakers and carriage store (and look out for the two pianos, including a baby grand). There are picnic tables out the front, and the pub extends a welcome to families, dogs, walkers and all-comers.

Crispin

Church Street. Tel (01246) 590591
Grid ref: 348633
Open: 12-3 (summer only), 7-11; 11-11 Sat; 12-10.30 Sun.

Beer: Mansfield Bitter, Riding Bitter; Marston's Pedigree.

Food: Traditional range of hot and cold pub food, including cobs and sandwiches, served 12-2.30 (when open) and 7-9 in no-smoking dining room and both bars.

Accommodation: B&B - 1 family, 1 double, 1 twin, 1 single.

General: Situated next to the church, the Crispin claims it is one of the oldest pubs in the Peak District, built in 1350 and supposedly licensed in 1416. Historical detail is provided by a sign on the outside front wall which explains amongst other things how Thomas Babington and "several men of Asher" returned victorious from the Battle of Agincourt (fought on St Crispin's Day, 1415). The double-fronted building is cosy and comfortable, a popular locals' pub, with two main bars, a dining room to the side and a family games/pool room to the rear. There is some outside seating, dogs are permitted in one bar, and families and walkers are made very welcome.

BAKEWELL - Derbyshire

So-called 'capital' of the Peak National Park, this honeypot town is well worth a nose around - but beware limited parking and congested roads, especially on market day (Monday). The town has one of the last remaining livestock markets in the Peak District, which takes place in the new Agricultural Centre on the eastern bank of the River Wye. Touristy shops abound, from woollens and whisky, to well-stocked out door gear retailers; plus there are numerous bakeries and tea shops, all of which serve the famous Bakewell Pudding. In order to walk off one of those sweet morsels, wander up to the imposing All Saints Parish Church, with its collection of Saxon crosses; and follow the signs around the corner for the fascinating Old House Museum, chocked full of curiosities. For further local details visit the Tourist Information Centre in the Old Market Hall, opposite the Co-op supermarket, tel (01629) 813227. Just to the north of the town is the popular Monsal Trail, a walking and cycling route; while two miles south along the A6, is the glorious Haddon Hall.

Castle Inn

Castle Street. Tel (01629) 812103
Grid ref: 218687
Open: 11-11; 12-10.30 Sun

Beer: Kelham Island Easy Rider; Marston's Pedigree; Boddingtons Bitter. Guest beers may include Charles Wells Bombadier;Timothy Taylor's Landlord; Castle Eden.

Food: Served 12-2, 6-8.30, in separate no-smoking dining area. Main menu includes bubble and squeak, cajun chicken, leek and Caerphilly cheese sausages, etc, plus light snacks and specials board.

Accommodation: B&B - 4 double rooms, all en-suite.

General: Previously called the Commercial and Castle, this 16th century inn by Bakewell's medieval bridge entertained a regular horse market for over 100 years. Its three garages, by the small outdoor patio seating area, were formally stables. Today the stone-flagged floor, wooden beams and tasteful lighting give the pub a warm and cosy feeling. Incidentally, nothing remains of the motte and bailey castle, which is supposed to have stood across the river on a small hill.

Medieval Bridge, Bakewell

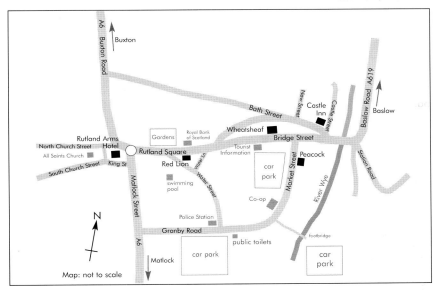

Peacock

Market Place. Tel (01629) 812994
Grid ref: 219686
Open: 11-11; 12-10.30 Sun.
Beer: Adnams Bitter; Greene King IPA; Tetley Bitter; Theakston's Best Bitter.
Food: Lunchtime and evening meals 'till 9.30pm (two rooms no-smoking).
Accommodation: B&B - 5 new en-suite rooms.
General: Bright, handsome 19th century pub near the Tourist Information Centre. Four separate rooms lead off from the one main bar, and outside there's a small area of patio seating (children welcome). Occasional live music at weekends. The peacock is the family crest of the Manners family (the Dukes of Rutland) of Haddon Hall.

Red Lion

The Square. Tel (01629) 812054
Grid ref: 218685
Open: 11-11; 12-10.30 Sun
Beer: Tetley Bitter; Theakston's Mild. Two guest beers, such as Courage Directors, Morland Speckled Hen.
Food: Meals and snacks, served in two bright bars and no-smoking dining area from noon to 8.30pm. Dishes may include breast of chicken in tarragon gravy, plus

fish, steaks, etc.
Accommodation: B&B - 4 double, 1 twin.
General: Originally thought to be a 16th century timber-framed inn, it's now a low, stone-built town centre pub, opposite Bath Gardens, at the far end of which sits Bath House. This is the only surviving reminder of the town's spa heritage. The spring supplied water at a constant 15°C, and was roofed over by the Duke of Rutland in 1697. There is a small beer garden to the rear of the pub. Children not allowed in bars after 9pm.

Bakewell Pudding

The town's famous export originated at the Rutland Arms Hotel back in the 1850s, due to the carelessness of the hotel cook. Intending to prepare a strawberry tart, she poured the mixture of eggs over the strawberry jam, instead of mixing it into the pastry, and what should have become a tart ended up a pudding. Luckily the result went down well with the guests, and a new culinary delicacy was established. Today the authentic recipe is still something of a secret jealously guarded by rival pudding shops - or so they would have you believe!

Central / Eastern

Rutland Arms Hotel, Bakewell

Rutland Arms Hotel

The Square. Tel (01629) 812812
Grid ref: 217684
Open: 11-11; 12-10.30 Sun.
Beer: Tetley Bitter; Greene King Abbot Ale.
Food: Lunchtime bar snacks (salads, baguettes, hot dishes) 12-2.15, and full evening menu (local lamb, venison etc.) in restaurant, 6.30-9. Extensive wine cellar. Smoking allowed in cocktail bar only.
Accommodation: B&B - 35 en-suite rooms, including some annex rooms.
General: Built in 1804, on the site of the former White Horse Inn, the Rutland Arms is an imposing Georgian construction, overlooking the town centre roundabout and main square. Opposite are the former stable blocks, now converted into extra accommodation. Jane Austen supposedly stayed at the Hotel in 1811, and according to some, used Bakewell as the model for the fictitious town of Lambton in 'Pride and Prejudice'.

> *Bakewell Farmers' Market: last Saturday in the month, at the Agricultural Centre*

Wheatsheaf

Bridge Street. Tel (01629) 812985
Grid ref: 218686
Open: 11-11; 12-10.30 Sun.
Beer: Mansfield Bitter; Banks's Bitter; Marston's Pedigree.
Food: Served 12-2, 6-9/9.30, all day at weekends, in spacious no-smoking dining room, or long, open bar. Daily specials, including up to half a dozen vegetarian dishes.
General: Until the 1950s the site was occupied by two pubs (the Anchor and

the Wheatsheaf), but Mansfield Brewery - who owned them both - perhaps rather inevitably knocked them into one. Disabled toilets; children welcome; limited outside seating by main door. Live music every Saturday evening, and at the weekend it's a popular venue with the younger drinkers, and tends to get very busy after 9pm.

BASLOW - Derbyshire

Located on the northern edge of Chatsworth Park, at the intersection of several key roads. This rather sprawling village is a useful base for exploring both Chatsworth (a short walk away from the car park at Goose Green) and the imposing gritstone 'edges' that line the moorland high above the Derwent valley. The river is spanned by a beautiful, triple-arched bridge, while the tower of the nearby Church of St Anne contains a clock, built to commemorate a former Queen's jubilee, which has 'VICTORIA 1897' arranged on the dial, instead of numbers.

Devonshire Arms

Nether End. Tel (01246) 582551
Grid ref: 259722
Open: 11-11; 12-10.30 Sun.
Beer: Bass; Marston's Pedigree.
Food: Meals and snacks served all day 'till 8.30/9. Popular carvery, plus changing specials board. Dining either in restaurant or bars, including no-smoking area.
Accommodation: B&B - 12 en-suite rooms (9 double, 2 twin and 1 single).
General: Large, family-friendly pub off A619 by the small triangle of Goose Green. Ramp at rear for wheelchair access, plus disabled toilet. No beer garden, but dogs welcome. Like the Cavendish and Wheatsheaf Hotels, the Devonshire was an important coaching inn and served the busy Buxton-Chesterfield turnpike.

Prince of Wales Hotel

Church Lane. Tel (01246) 582115
Grid ref: 254724
Open: 12-3, 7-11; 12-3, 7-10.30 Sun.
Beer: Bass; Stones Bitter.
Food: Full range of snacks and meals served 12-2, 7-9, either in bar or no-smoking restaurant. Includes Sunday roast,

children's menu, etc.

Accommodation: B&B - 3 en-suite doubles.

General: Dark, snug 18th century coaching house adjoining churchyard, and run for the last 20 years by former professional footballer Bernard Shaw (Wolves, Sheffield Wednesday, and England). Families welcome. Special wheelchair entrance at front. Dogs permitted inside.

Rutland Arms

Calver Road. Tel (01246) 582276
Grid ref 253724
Open: 12-3, 6-11 (11-11 summer) 11-11 Sat;
12-10.30 Sun.

Beer: Mansfield Bitter; Marston's Pedigree or Banks's Bitter, and one guest beer.

Food: Light snacks and meals from set menu or specials board, served 12-3, 6-9, weekends all day 'till 9pm. One of the bars is no-smoking.

Accommodation: B&B - 3 bedrooms.

General: Originally called the Green Man. The pub stands next to the old stone bridge over the Derwent, beside which sits the former tollbooth (opposite is Toll Bar Cottage). Beer garden and patio by the river; children welcome; real fires; pool table.

Wheatsheaf Hotel

Nether End. Tel (01246) 582240
Grid ref: 259723
Open: 11-11; 12-10.30 Sun.

Beer: Banks's Bitter; Mansfield Bitter; Marston's Pedigree.

Food: Snacks and meals served 11.30-9.30 Mon-Sat, 12-8 Sun. The pub is particularly renowned for its pies, including home-made steak pie, as well as minty lamb, and chicken, ham and leek pie. Dine in a choice of bars, including no-smoking area.

Accommodation: B&B - 5 bedrooms (3 en-suite): 3 twins, 2 doubles.

General: No dogs inside, and children in dining area only, but beer garden includes play area and climbing frame. Warm, cosy interior, and popular eating place. But if you choose B&B, beware! One of the rooms is supposedly haunted by an ostler, who occasionally makes the journey across a long disappeared bridge from the courtyard stables to the main building.

BEELEY - Derbyshire

Beeley is a small estate village lying just to the south of Chatsworth. Opposite the church a fieldpath leads to the 1,000-acre Chatsworth Park, the centrepiece of which is the stunning House. Originally Elizabethan, it's been extensively remodelled over the last 400 years by generations of the Cavendish family, and is surrounded by beautiful gardens (including fountains, a waterfall, and a maze). A more demanding approach on foot from Beeley is across the moors above the village. The moor contains a prehistoric burial mound known as Hob Hurst's House, where the elf 'Hob i'th'Hurst' supposedly resides.

Access: 3 miles east of Bakewell (off B6012).

Devonshire Arms, Beeley

Devonshire Arms

Beeley. Tel (01629) 733259
Grid ref: 265675
Open: 11-11; 12-10.30 Sun.

Beer: Black Sheep Best Bitter, Special Ale; Theakston's XB, Old Peculier, plus a guest beer.

Food: Meals and bar snacks served 'till 9.30, including a 'Victorian Breakfast' each Sunday morning, and a special fish menu every Friday. Other dishes include Fillet Steak Balmoral, black pudding and bacon salad, and smoked haddock rarebit. Pub includes no-smoking restaurant and bar.

General: This attractive village inn was opened in 1747, after three cottages were knocked into one. A long, dark low building, with oak beams and real fires, decent real ales, and a refreshing absence of modern pub clutter. Family-friendly; walkers welcome; patio seating outside.

BIRCHOVER - Derbyshire

This pleasant village known locally as 'Bircher' is tucked away on the southern slopes of Stanton Moor amid some impressive rock country. There are several notable outcrops, such as nearby Robin Hood's Stride and Cratcliff Tor, plus a number of intriguing boulders that dot the edge of the moor itself. Up here, amongst the heather and the silver birch, you'll find Nine Ladies Stone Circle and a host of Bronze Age burial mounds and tumuli. Beside the Druid Inn is a short path up to Rowtor Rocks, where 300 years ago Rev. Thomas Eyre carved steps and seats into the gritstone. More at www.birchovervillage.co.uk.
Access: 5 miles south-east of Bakewell (off B5056).

Druid Inn

Birchover. Tel (01629) 650302
Grid ref 236622
Open: 12-2, 7-11; 12-2, 7-10.30 Sun.
Beer: Mansfield Bitter; Marston's Pedigree, plus house beer Druid Ale (subject to availability) brewed for the pub by the Leatherbritches Brewery; see Bentley Brook Inn (Peak District South).
Food: The Druid Inn has a large and impressively varied menu chalked up on a vast blackboard by the main bar. Served lunchtime and evening, it includes the likes of Derbyshire pheasant & lamb stew, steak & mussel pie, and halibut baked with orange, ginger and garlic; plus there's an extensive vegetarian menu and full wine list. Call ahead to check serving times and book a table - especially at weekends.
General: The Druid Inn is primarily a food pub, comprising a small bar area and taproom, and several dining rooms (no-smoking). However, there is outdoor seating on the terrace beneath the main building's ivy-clad exterior. Children in dining area if eating (until 8.30pm).

Red Lion

Main Street. Tel (01629) 650363
Grid ref: 236622
Open: 12-2, 7-11 (11-11 Sat summer); 12-10.30 Sun.
Beer: Mansfield Bitter; Marston's Pedigree,

plus two guest beers (such as Bateman's Excalibur, Offilers Best Derby Beer, Shepherd Neame Spitfire).
Food: Bar snacks at lunchtime only, including 'Quarryman's Lunch' - the village's early growth was as much due to local gritstone as the plough.
General: Pleasant, welcoming village pub built in 1680, fronted by south-facing yard, with picnic tables. Two comfortable bars, the smaller one incorporating a 30 ft deep well which was originally the building's water supply. Occasional live music at weekends. Family-friendly, but no children after 9pm. Walkers welcome.

BONSALL - Derbyshire

Half hidden between Masson Hill and the wooded chasm of Via Gellia, Bonsall is a rather strung out sort of place, but still well worth exploring - not least because of its two good pubs. The old market cross, which sits on 13 concentric steps outside the King's Head, dates from 1628 and was once the venue for bull baiting (the original ring is in the village church). In the last few years Bonsall has made national news for its UFO connection - apparently there have been numerous and unexplained 'sightings' in the night sky over the village!
Access: 2 miles west of Matlock (off A5012).

Barley Mow

The Dale. Tel (01629) 825685
Grid ref: 275581
Open: 6 (11 Sat)-11; 12-10.30 Sun.
Beer: Whim Hartington Bitter; Greene King Abbot Ale; Kimberley Bitter (electric pump dispense); plus up to two guest beers.
Food: Small but appetising range of traditional home-cooked meals (evenings only), including vegetarian options.
General: Richly decorated and cosy one bar pub, with garden at back and inviting terrace out front (families welcome). The jovial landlord leads local walks each Bank Holiday, and over 3,500 have taken part over the last six years. Live music Saturday evening with impromptu sessions. The pub also featured in the recent best selling novel 'Pastures Nouveaux' by Wendy Holden. (A 'barley mow' is a rick of barley from which ale used to be brewed.)

King's Head, Bonsall

King's Head

Yeoman Street. Tel (01629) 822703

Grid ref: 278583

Open: 12-3, 6-11; 12-3, 6-10.30 Sun.

Beer: Bateman's XB, Dark Mild, Bateman's seasonal beers.

Food: Full range of snacks and meals served 12-2.15/2.30, 6.30-8.30.

General: Although a beam near the window is signed by the first landlord's son, Anthony Abell, and dated 1677, the pub is thought to have been built in 1649 - hence the head of the king in question is probably Charles I (which is perhaps surprising as this was mostly a Parliamentary stronghold during the Civil War). It's a dark and cosy village inn, whose two wood-panelled bars include open fires, darts board and gaming table. Families welcome; limited outside seating.

CHELMORTON - Derbyshire

A high village (1,000 ft) lying under the shadow of Chelmorton Low, whose bulky hillside contains two Neolithic tumuli. Many of the buildings retain their original fields, and these distinctive narrow walled strips (known as the 'infield') date back to the Middle Ages and are now carefully protected. The local stream, that runs down Chelmorton's single street only to disappear into the porous limestone, is known as the Illy Willy Water.

Access: 4 miles south-east of Buxton.

Church Inn

Chelmorton. Tel (01298) 85319

Grid ref: 115704

Open: 12-3.30, 7-11 (11-11 Sat summer); 12-3.30, 7-10.30 (12-10.30 summer) Sun.

Beer: Adnams Bitter; Marston's Bitter, Pedigree, one guest beer, such as Morland Old Speckled Hen; Timothy Taylor's Landlord.

Food: Freshly made snacks and meals seved 12-2, 7-9, such as breast of chicken with stilton sauce, home made steak and kidney pie, chicken jalfrezi.

General: Inn was originally known as the Blacksmith's Arms, reflecting the dual profession of an earlier landlord. This friendly pub at the far end of the village street comprises one long, knocked-through bar and a side room with pool table. Plenty of picnic table seating in the open yard, which faces the Church of St John the Baptist (look out for the locust weathervane, symbolising his time in the

17

Central / Eastern

wilderness). Children welcome up to 9pm. Occasional live music at weekends.

DARLEY BRIDGE - Derbyshire

Situated off the Winster road, midway between Darley Dale and Wensley, the small community has grown up by the historic bridge over the Derwent. The imposing river rises on the open moors of Bleaklow, above Howden Reservoir, to flow the length of the National Park, joining the River Trent near Nottingham.

Access: 2 miles north-west of Matlock (on B5057).

Square and Compass

Darley Bridge. Tel (01629) 733255
Grid ref: 271622
Open: 11-11; 12-10.30 Sun.
Beer: Robinson's Best Bitter, plus Robinson's seasonal beer.
Food: Extensive choice of meals and snacks, served in main bar or no-smoking restaurant 12-2, 6-9. Specialities include seasonal oysters, game dishes, and various curries.
Accommodation: B&B - 5 en-suite rooms, including two family rooms. Private camping and caravan site on land opposite.
General: Extended, 18th century pub opposite the bridge, with two separate beer gardens. Live music every week, plus the new owners are hoping to hold outdoor entertainment over the summer. Families and walkers welcome; wheelchair access to restaurant. The pub also holds fishing rights to 300 yards of the Derwent - anglers welcome!

Three Stags Heads

Darley Bridge. Tel (01629) 732358
Grid ref: 269629
Open: 12-3, 6.30/7-11 (11-11 summer); 11-11 Sat; 12-3, 6.30/7-10.30 (12-10.30 summer) Sun.
Beer: Kimberley Best Bitter, Mild, plus Kimberley seasonal beers.
Food: Daily menu (12-2, 7-8.30), including children's options and vegetarian list, plus changing specials board (such as vegetable stroganoff, and lamb casserole with mint dumplings).
General: Listed building (1735), comprising two well furnished bars with open fire.

There are two large beer gardens (a children's adventure playground is planned), and the landlord reports that wild deer sometimes come into the garden to feed - three stags, perhaps? Walkers are very welcome. Above the main door are carved the letters 'GOQ', which apparently stand for 'Go Out Quietly'.

> "There is no finer county in England than Derbyshire. To sit in the shade on a fine day and look upon verdure is the most perfect refreshment." Jane Austen

DARLEY DALE - Derbyshire

The name Darley Dale tends to describe the loose cluster of villages (including Northwood, Churchtown and Two Dales) which are grouped above the Derwent's eastern bank between Matlock and Rowsley. It's home to Peak Rail, who run steam outings in holiday periods. The Darley Yew, next to the 12th century St Helen's church, is a massive, gnarled old tree whose 33-ft girth makes it one of the oldest yews in Britain.

Access: off A6 north of Matlock.

Church Inn

Church Road, Churchtown. Tel (01298) 732291
Grid ref: 267633
Open: 5.30-11 Mon-Tue; 12-3, 5.30-11 Wed-Thu; 11-11 Fri-Sat; 12-10.30 Sun.
Beer: Kimberley Best Bitter, plus one occasional Kimberley seasonal beer.
Food: Snacks only (such as toasties), when open.
General: Compact and pleasant locals' pub by Church Lane level crossing (follow signs for parish church). It's the base for a club dedicated to vintage motor vehicles, and each summer shows are held in the car park opposite (they feature vintage lorries, fire engines etc). Beer garden at back; dogs permitted in tap room only; children welcome in summer months.

Grouse Inn

Dale Road North (A6) (01298) 734357
Grid ref: 268634
Open: 12-3, 7-11 Mon-Thu; 11-11 Fri-Sat; 12-10.30 Sun.
Beer: Kimberley Best Bitter, plus Kimberley

seasonal beer.

Food: Served 12-3, 6-9 in one open plan bar. Separate meals and light snacks menus, with daily specials board.

General: Family-friendly pub on main Matlock-Bakewell road, with beer garden at rear containing an adventure playground and boules pitch (children not allowed in the bar after 8.30pm). Pool room and open fire, dogs permitted inside. Wheelchair access via side door to bar, and back gates to garden. Live bands every Saturday night, and jazz performances last Sunday of each month.

Plough

Wheatley Road, Two Dales. Tel (01629) 732260
Grid ref: 282630
Open: 12-2, 6-11 (11-11 summer); 12-2, 6-10.30 (12-10.30 summer) Sun.

Beer: Tetley Bitter; Greene King Abbot Ale; Morland Old Speckled Hen; Marston's Pedigree, plus two guest beers (such as Timothy Taylor's Landlord; Brakspear Bitter, etc).

Food: Appetising home cooked food every lunchtime and evenings (except Sun eve) 'till 8.30, including specials such as escalope parmesan (pork or chicken fillets in breadcrumbs topped with spicy, three cheese sauce).

Accommodation: Campsite.

General: Friendly, undisturbed local (built 1751), tucked away but well worth locating (off Darley Dale-Chesterfield road). Two cosy bars, plus pool room, and a huge open-lawned space at rear with picnic tables, a children's climbing frame, and campsite. The pub has its own football, darts, pool and boules teams, and is home to the Panthers Motorbike Club (classic bikes).

Whitworth Hotel

Dale Road North (A6). Tel (01629) 733568
Grid ref: 275628
Open: 11-11; 12-10.30 Sun.

Beer: Mansfield Bitter.

Food: Range of traditional meals and snacks, including Sunday roast, served in bar or no-smoking dining room, 12-2 and early/mid evening.

Accommodation: B&B - 6 en-suite rooms (5 double, 1 twin), including 1 family room.

General: Although run separately, this imposing, Grade II listed building sits next to the equally grand Joseph Whitworth Centre (or Institute). The buildings and the adjoining ten acre park are named after the renowned Victorian industrialist, who amongst other things invented the standard screw thread and the Whitworth Rifle. He also owned the nearby Stancliffe quarries which provided the paving stones for Trafalgar Square. A ramp is available for wheelchair access; no children after 7.30pm.

EARL STERNDALE - Derbyshire

Popular with walkers, this high and rather isolated village is bordered to the south and west by the glorious limestone scenery of the Upper Dove valley, close to Parkhouse and Chrome Hill.

Access: 4 miles south-east of Buxton (off B5053).

The Quiet Woman, Earl Sterndale

Quiet Woman

Earl Sterndale. Tel (01298) 83211
Grid ref: 091669
Open: 11-3, 7-11; 12-3, 7-10.30 Sun.

Beer: Marston's Bitter; Marston's Pedigree, plus one guest beer such as Whim Hartington; Everards Tiger, or beers from Beartown brewery of Congleton.

Food: Toasties and occasional winter hotpot only; plus local pork pies, cheeses and eggs (from pub's own hens).

Accommodation: Caravan and campsite in field at rear.

General: Externally rather plain, but inside this unpretentious, one-bar village local there's a welcome lack of modern frills. No jukebox or bowls of chips, but genuine oak beams (the pub dates from 1615), tiled floor and real fire - and you can even enjoy your drink at a former laying-out table (purchased from an undertaker). Children in pool/games room only; live music most Sundays (folk, country and western, Appalachian); no dogs inside; small beer garden. Finally, the name: 'Soft words turneth away wrath' is the motto below the pub sign depicting a headless woman. Apparently a former landlord returned from market at nearby Longnor, and fed up with his wife's constant nagging determined to have a quiet woman outside rather than in.

EASTMOOR - Derbyshire

A hamlet high up on the eastern moors of the Peak District, on the Chesterfield-Baslow road (A619).

Highwayman

Baslow Road (A619). Tel (01246) 566330
Grid ref: 306714
Open: 11-11; 12-10.30 Sun.
Beer: Marston's Pedigree.
Food: Extensive set menu (from salads and baguettes to steaks and roasts) served 12-10pm daily.
Accommodation: B&B - 7 rooms (3 single, 2 double, 1 twin, 1 family room).
General: Large Brewsters pub situated on the busy road from Chesterfield. Its open, spacious bars are very popular with families, especially since there's a supervised 'fun factory' for children (open until 9pm). Attractive courtyard patio, and separate garden seating with good views over the moors. Rail ramp access and disabled toilets. No dogs permitted.

ELTON - Derbyshire

A former leadmining village, today Elton is a quiet backwater with a highly individual pub. After winter snowfall, skiing sometimes takes place on the adjoining fields when the villagers erect a drag lift.
Access: Half way between Bakewell and Matlock (off B5056).

Duke of York

Main Street. Tel (01269) 650367
Grid ref: 223609
Open: 8.30-11 (closed Mon-Sat lunchtimes); 12-3, 8.30-10.30 Sun.

Beer: Mansfield Bitter; Adnams Bitter.
General: The landlady of 30 years has kept this sedate, unfussy building almost entirely free of modern trappings: no pub food, no music, no beer garden. The two front rooms are like Victorian parlours, with period fireplaces and rather austere furniture; but the tiny, cosy tap room is the real gem, with its tiled floor and open fire, low-hung bar and corridor hatch. The pub extends a welcome to everyone – families, dog-owners, walkers, and so on.

"What contemptible scoundrel stole the cork from my lunch?" W C Fields

FLAGG - Derbyshire

Situated on the high and exposed limestone plateau between Buxton and Bakewell, the rather strung-out hamlet of Flagg is famous for its point-to-point race meeting held on Easter Tuesday, a lively steeplechase where walls are used as jumps.
Access: 6 miles south east of Buxton (off A515).

Plough Inn

Flagg. Tel (01298) 85557
Grid ref: 138684
Open: 12-3, 7-11; 12-10.30 Sun.
Beer: Marston's Pedigree; Black Sheep Best Bitter, plus one guest beer (summer only).
Food: Served in bar or no-smoking restaurant 12-2, 7-9. Choice of the lunchtime carvery or sandwiches, and full evening menu which may includes dishes such as pheasant in red wine, swordfish, salmon, plus vegetarian options and children's choices.
Accommodation: B&B - 2 en-suite rooms (double and twin), with more rooms planned in the future.
General: Dating back to 1847, and variously called the Star, and the Angel, this welcoming family-run pub offers a comfortable main bar and refurbished carvery/dining room (with a resident caged macaw). There's also a games room featuring bar billiards, pool, darts and bar skittles, plus an old-fashioned jukebox. Families and children are welcome, as are dog owners, and there's a beer garden for the summer months.

GRANGEMILL - Derbyshire

A hamlet by the junction of the A5012 (Newhaven-Cromford) and B5056 (Ashbourne-Bakewell), and four miles southwest of Matlock.

Hollybush Inn

Grangemill. Tel (01629) 650300
Grid ref: 244577
Open: 11-11; 12-10.30 Sun.
Beer: Marston's Pedigree.
Food: Full range of meals and snacks served lunchtime and evenings 'till around 10pm, either in comfortable main bar or no-smoking restaurant, including chidren's menu and Sunday roast.
General: A large, detached building at the head of Via Gellia, formerly believed to be a farm and coaching inn, and also used for a time as an overnight holding cell for prisoners being transported to Manchester! There's a warmer reception for today's visitors: log fires, beer garden, plus a games room for children. Walkers welcome; dogs permitted inside.

GREAT LONGSTONE - Derbyshire

An attractive, one-street village sheltering below the dominant ridge of Longstone Edge (from where there are great views over the southern/central part of the National Park). A traditional local trade is reflected in the name of the main pub, since St Crispin is the patron saint of shoemakers - and according to legend such was his benevolence he stole leather in order to make shoes for the poor.

Crispin Inn

Main Street. Tel (01629) 640237
Grid ref: 198718
Open: 12-2.30, 6-11; 11.30-3, 6-11 Sat;
12-3.30, 6-10.30 Sun.
Beer: Robinson's Best Bitter, Old Stockport Bitter, Robinson's seasonal beer.
Food: Good range of snacks and full meals served 12-2, 6.30-9, throughout the pub. The landlord used to be a butcher, and still cures his own pork for gammon and boils his hams, so not surprisingly the likes of steak, beef and ale pie, and so on, are a speciality here. No smoking in part of

main bar, dining room and function room.
Accommodation: Nearby cottage (sleeps 4) let on a B&B or self catering basis.
General: Large, comfortable old pub with one spacious, open bar and separate dining room and newly-built function room. Open fire; beer garden at side; families welcome, but no dogs inside.

HASSOP - Derbyshire

The centrepiece of this leafy hamlet is Hassop Hall, former seat of the Eyres of Hassop, and now an exclusive hotel and restaurant.
Access: 2 miles north of Bakewell (on B6001).

Eyre Arms

Hassop. Tel (01629) 640390
Grid ref: 225724
Open: 11.30-3, 6-11; 12-3, 6-10.30 Sun.
Beer: Black Sheep Best Bitter; Marston's Pedigree; John Smith's Bitter.
Food: Served 12-2, 6-9, the varied and entirely home-made menu contains such delicacies as monkfish, rabbit pie, and Huntsman's Pot (venison, rabbit, etc), plus vegetarian options like bulgar wheat and walnut casserole. No smoking in lounge and snug bar.
General: Handsome, 17th century inn decorated in climbing vines, with a pleasant walled garden to the side. The peaceful, tastefully furnished interior contains a huge coat of arms belonging to the original Rowland Eyre, a Royalist officer in the Civil War. He raised a regiment in Derbyshire and fought at the Battle of Marston Moor. An escaping Cavalier, captured in a 'priest hole' in the pub, is said to still haunt the premises to this day! Accompanied children welcome if eating; sorry, no dogs.

HURDLOW - Derbyshire

A hamlet close to the Ashbourne-Buxton road, and at the northern end of the popular High Peak Trail, which together with the linking Tissington Trail offer miles of scenic traffic-free walking and cycling along former railway lines.
Access: 6 miles south-east of Buxton (off A515).

Hurdlow – Little Longstone

Central / Eastern

Bull i' th' Thorn, Hurdlow

Bull i' th' Thorn

Ashbourne Road (A515). Tel (01298) 83348
Grid ref: 128666

Open: 11-11; 12-10.30 Sun.

Beer: Robinson's Best Bitter, Hartleys Fellrunner.

Food: Mouthwatering choice of snacks and main meals, from traditional to the more exotic (wild boar steak, medallions of ostrich). Daily specials board regularly includes salmon, trout, and other fish. Served in main bar or medieval banquet room, all day 'till 9pm.

Accommodation: B&B - 3 en-suite doubles including two 4-poster rooms. Campsite in adjoining field.

General: Fascinating, historic building standing alone by the main road - the original farmstead is believed to be 12th century, and the pub dates from 1472. Atmospheric, oak-panelled bar with open fire, plus suits of armour, carvings, stuffed bear's head, resident ghosts, etc. Welcoming owners offer families the choice of a separate children's room, plus fort, climbing frame and animal farm by beer garden. Function room and campsite regularly plays host to rallies and various club meetings.

Royal Oak

Hurdlow/Sparklow. Tel (01298) 83288
Grid ref: 126659

Open: 11-11; 12-10.30 Sun.

Beer: Marston's Pedigree; Worthington Bitter, plus one guest beer (such as Bass; Whim Hartington Bitter, etc).

Food: Hot and cold meals served 12-9 daily. Home-made food includes traditional pies (beef and stilton, etc). Well-priced steak night every Thurs (beef, gammon, pork,

fish, quorn, etc).

Accommodation: Camping & bunkhouse.

General: Friendly, well positioned pub near car park for High Peak Trail (above former railway bridge, marked as 'Sparklow' on OS White Peak map). Welcomes walkers, cyclists and all-comers, plus families, and well behaved dogs. Small main bar with open fire, lower dining area, plus separate public bar with pool table. Beer garden gives open views over fields. Occasional impromptu Saturday night music (cajun, folk).

---

cask: a generic term for a beer barrel

LITTLE LONGSTONE - Derbyshire

The smaller of the two Longstone villages is situated on the Monsal Trail, an 8 mile walking/cycling route that links Bakewell with Wyedale, near Buxton, and for the most part follows the course of Midland Railway's former London-Manchester line.

Access: 2 miles north-west of Bakewell (off B6465).

Packhorse Inn

Main Street. Tel (01629) 640471
Grid ref: 190717

Open: 11.30-2.30/3, 5-11; 12-10.30 Sun.

Beer: Marston's Pedigree, Bitter.

Food: Meals and snacks served lunchtime and evening, with a specials board that may include steak and stilton pie, and lamb steaks with redcurrant and rosemary.

General: This attractive, traditional stone building began as two or three miners' cottages (c1600), and became a pub in 1787. The rooms are small and cosy, simply furnished, and apart from welcoming families and dogs it's also a walker/cyclist-friendly establishment on the Monsal Trail (see above). There's a tiny, terraced garden at the rear where occasional summer barbecues are held (bring your own food). The pub hosts folk sessions every Wednesday evening (free).

Lo! The poor toper whose untutored sense,
Sees bliss in ale, and can never with wine dispense;
Whose head proud and fancy never taught to steer
Beyond the muddy ecstasies of beer.

George Crabbe

LITTON - Derbyshire

Located a mile east of Tideswell, Litton is another quiet and attractive village of traditional limestone cottages and houses, with the pub just off the main green. From here it's a short walk across fields to Tansley Dale and the sheltered, flower-rich slopes of Cressbrook Dale.

Access: 5 miles north-west of Bakewell (off A623).

Red Lion, Litton

Red Lion

Main Street. Tel (01298) 871458
Grid ref: 164753
Open: 11.30-4, 6-11 Mon-Thu; 11-11 Fri-Sat; 12-10.30 Sun.
Beer: Jennings Cumberland Ale; Barnsley Bitter, plus two guest beers (Tetley Bitter; Oakwells Old Tom etc).
Food: Appetising hot and cold food served 12-2, 6-8/8.30 (not Sun) throughout the pub (back room no-smoking). Apart from the standard choices of light snacks and meals, home-made specials include garlic lamb, moussaka in red wine sauce, and Bobotie (a South African dish of minced lamb and apricot in red wine).
General: A delightful, cosy village pub, made up of three 17th century cottages and still retaining an intimate and well preserved feel (low ceilings, open fires, subtle lighting). As well as organising the Litton Music Life Festival, occasional jazz and folk sessions are held here. No children under six, some front seating on the village green outside. Dogs allowed inside.

> *"What two ideas are more inseparable than beer and Britannia"* Sydney Smith

MATLOCK - Derbyshire

Although outside the National Park boundary, Matlock is a busy and popular centre from which to explore the Peak District. About 150 years ago it became well known as a spa town. There were as many as 30 so-called hydros offering restorative water treatments and cures. One of the most popular, was John Smedley's Hydro, and since closing in 1955 this imposing building off Bank Road has become the offices of Derbyshire County Council. On the hilltop to the south is the stark silhouette of Riber Castle, built in the 1850s by Smedley as his private residence. For further details on what to see and do in and around Matlock, visit the Tourist Information Centre on Crown Square, tel (01629) 583388.

> *Kil or kilderkin: an 18-gallon cask*

Boat House

110 Dale Road. Tel (01629) 583776
Grid ref: 297598
Open: 11-11; 12-10.30 Sun.
Beer: Kimberley Best Bitter, Mild, plus Kimberley seasonal beer.
Food: Tasty meals and snacks served lunchtime and evening (until 9pm), 12-4 on Sunday. Specialises in fresh seafood and shellfish (sea bass, salmon, mussels, oysters, lobster, trout, etc), either on their own or in specific seafood platters - described as "a gourmet feast for the fish and shellfish connoisseur." Food served either in the two bars or two no-smoking dining rooms.
Accommodation: B&B - 5 rooms (1 single, 2 double, 2 twin).
General: Situated off the A6, between Matlock and Matlock Bath (just beyond the railway bridge) this welcoming establishment offers tastefully furnished bars, an open fire, children's room and some outside seating. Dogs are allowed inside. Pleasure craft and rowing boats were once built in the car park area (hence the pub's name) at a time when there was even a ferry across the nearby River Derwent. Almost 300 years old, in its time the building has also been used as a mortuary and a brothel!

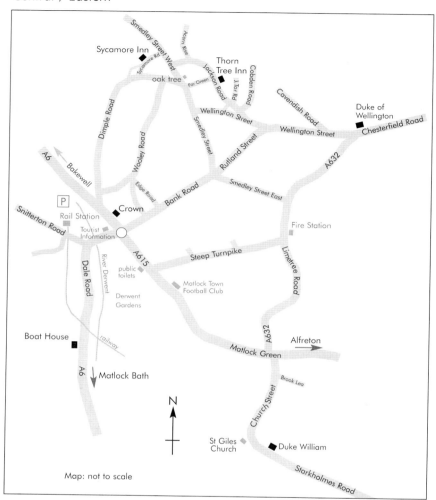

Map: not to scale

Crown

Derwent House, Crown Square.
Tel (01629) 580991
Grid ref: 298603
Open: 11-11; 12-10.30 Sun.
Beer: Six regular beers (including Theakston's Old Peculier; Courage Directors; Marston's Pedigree and Shepherd Neame Spitfire), plus two guest beers, most at discounted prices.
Food: Set menu of snacks and meals, served all day. There is a large no-smoking area (including at bar); extensive wine list.
General: Modern and busy J D Wetherspoon's pub by town centre roundabout, built on the site of two former shops. Large, open-plan design on pavement level, providing easy wheelchair access. No children; no dogs (except guide dogs). Occasional beer festivals and other events.

Duke of Wellington

115 Wellington Street. Tel (01629) 582299
Grid ref: 307608
Open: 11.30-2.30/3, 5.30/6-11;
12-2.30/3, 7-10.30 Sun.
Beer: Kimberley Best Bitter, plus Kimberley seasonal beer.

Food: Modest but decent range of good, home-cooked food, served every lunchtime, including Sunday roast, at reasonable prices.

Accommodation: B&B - 3 rooms (1 single, 2 double).

General: Located near the top of the hill, off Chesterfield Road (A632) this solid little building contains a series of small and attractive open rooms grouped around a central bar (wooden beams, arched doorways, real fire, etc). Picnic tables outside front, and more at rear in beer garden (lawn has children's climbing frame). No children after 9pm; dogs in tap room only.

Duke William

91 Church Street. Tel (01629) 582585
Grid ref: 298603
Open: 11(5 Mon)-11; 12-10.30 Sun.
Beer: Marston's Pedigree; Mansfield Dark Mild, Bitter; Banks's Bitter, plus one guest beer.
Food: Popular range of traditional dishes (steak and ale pie, cod and chips, etc), with changing specials board - served lunchtime and evenings (7-8.30, except Thurs). Advisable to book for Sunday carvery (12-3). Food served throughout the pub, but lounge and family dining area no-smoking.
Accommodation: Camping in field to rear.
General: Large, comfortable and tastefully decorated pub, situated just outside the centre of town near the parish church (known as 'Old Matlock'- the original settlement). Built in 1754, the listed building is named after the Duke of Devonshire of Chatsworth. It's a family-friendly place, with outdoor climbing frame and slides, garden and picnic tables, and children's toilets. Popular with walkers and groups. Bar skittles in public bar, plus piano and occasional live music.

Sycamore Inn

Sycamore Road (off Smedley Street West/Dimple Road). Tel (01629) 57585
Grid ref: 296608
Open: 11.30 (12 Sat)-2.30 (4 Sat), 7.30-11; 12-4, 7.30-10.30 Sun.
Beer: Bass; Fuller's London Pride, plus one guest beer.

Food: Well-priced lunchtime snacks - eat-in or take-away - include grilled panninis (spicy salami, roast beef and onions, mozzarella courgette), plus full meals from separate evening menu. Served 12-2 (3 at weekends), 6-9 (7-9 Sun).

General: Situated high up on Matlock's residential northern slopes (turn left on to Smedley Street West, by the council offices), this modest, unspoilt pub contains two small but tastefully decorated bars, including a recently uncovered fireplace of considerable antiquity. To the rear there's a boules pitch and beer garden, plus a children's play area and swings. Dogs allowed inside.

Thorn Tree Inn

48 Jackson Road (off Smedley Street West). Tel (01629) 582923
Grid ref: 299608
Open: 12-2.30, 7-11; 12-10.30 Sun.
Beer: Three changing real ales, such as Whim Hartington Bitter; Burton Bridge Bitter and beers from the Black Sheep Brewery.
Food: Well-priced, home cooked food, served 12-2, 7-8.30 daily.
General: A little gem of a pub, tucked away among Matlock's steep northern back streets. There are two small and intimate bars (smoke room and public bar), richly decorated with all sorts of memorabilia, including an upright piano. Out the front is a heated terrace with tables that offer glorious views over the town and Darley Dale. In the summer there are barbecues, and twice a year the pub holds a beer festival with eight or nine racked beers on offer. Occasional music; no children inside.

MATLOCK BATH - Derbyshire

Matlock Bath occupies the foot of a dramatic limestone gorge downriver from Matlock. With its waterside promenade, amusement arcades and ice cream kiosks, it almost has the air of a seaside resort. The former spa town has a range of attractions - from Gulliver's Kingdom and the Heights of Abraham (with its caverns and cable car) to a slalom canoe course on the

Central / Eastern

Derwent, and Derbyshire Wildlife Trust's Whistlestop Centre next to the railway station. In the autumn the riverside gardens host annual Illuminations, including the so-called 'Venetian Nights' when illuminated boats ply the river. For more information contact the Tourist Information Centre at the Pavillion, Matlock Bath, tel (01629) 55082.

Taking the Waters

The popularity of Matlock Bath's thermal springs really began with the arrival of the railway in the 1840s. For a short while hydrotherapy was the in-thing and trainloads flocked to the hydros of both Matlock Bath and neighbouring Matlock, to sample the local water. (You were required not just to bathe in it, but also drink great volumes of the stuff every day.) Matlock Bath has five thermal springs, four of which rise at a temperature of around 20°C/68°F, and water analysis has revealed that it does indeed contain plenty of elements essential for good health, such as iodine and fluoride. There were also a number of so-called petrifying wells, which could be entered for a small fee, to view the various items gradually being encrusted by the limestone rich water. Unfortunately the success of the baths, hydros and wells was short-lived, and by the 1940s they had nearly all shut down. Today most of the spring water is simply piped into the Derwent. (For more details see 'The Thermal Springs of Matlock Bath' by Allan Pentecost, available from the Tourist Information Centre.)

Fishpond

South Parade. Tel (01629) 581000
www.fishpond.co.uk
Grid ref: 293582
Open: 11-11; 12-10.30 Sun.
Beer: Bass; Morland Old Speckled Hen.
Food: Bar snacks and meals, served in either bar, lunchtime and evening (part of main bar is no-smoking) and from 12-9 at weekends.
General: Justly famous live music pub

features two bars, pool room, outside forecourt seating and a small garden, plus a stylish upstairs ballroom (230 capacity) with arched ceiling and sprung dancefloor. The Fishpond puts on at least two gigs a week, plus the 'Sunday Session' in the bar, and regularly features well-known names from the world of folk and rock, as well as local acts. It also has its own 4-CD set of groups and artists recorded live at the pub.

Midland

North Parade. Tel (01629) 582630
Grid ref: 296584
Open: 12-2.30, 7-11 (11-11 summer);
12-2.30, 7-11 (12-10.30 summer) Sun.
Beer: Tetley Bitter; Marston's Pedigree.
Food: Usual range of meals and snacks served 12-3, 7-9, either in main bar or no-smoking conservatory.
General: Located by the bridge over the Derwent leading to Matlock Bath Station, the pub has a wonderfully sited river garden and terrace with ample seating (but of course very popular in the holiday season). Children and families welcome: dogs permitted inside.

MILLER'S DALE - Derbyshire

Just along from the Angler's Rest are two mighty viaducts that once carried the London-Manchester railway across the plunging dale. In its time this was a bustling junction, for apart from the expresses there was a branch line to Buxton and frequent goods trains serving the local quarries and lime works. Today you can cross the viaducts on foot via the Monsal Trail - access via the former Miller's Dale station (car park, toilets, visitor information).
Access: 5 miles east of Buxton on B6049.

Angler's Rest

Miller's Dale. Tel (01298) 871323
Grid ref: 143734
Open: 12-3, 6.30-11; 12-3, 6.30-10.30 Sun.
Beer: Tetley Bitter; Marston's Pedigree; Fuller's London Pride, plus one guest beer.
Food: A traditional, changing menu of snacks and full meals, seved lunchtime and evening ('till 9pm) in two bars or no-smoking restaurant. Main dishes include

steaks, trout fillet, chicken and leek suet pudding, cod and prawn crumble.

General: Pleasant pub, close to the river in the quiet, leafy depths of Miller's Dale, south of Tideswell. The vine-covered building dates from the 1750s and used to be called the Peacock. It has a Hiker's Bar for booted visitors (the Limestone Way and Monsal Trail pass nearby), plus a lounge bar with open fire and richly decorated dining room - look out for the collection of Toby jugs. Children welcome up 'till 9pm; dogs in Hiker's Bar only; outside seating.

Angler's Rest, Miller's Dale

MONSAL HEAD - Derbyshire

One of the Peak District's best known viewpoints, Monsal Head overlooks the picturesque River Wye as it winds its way out of the steep sided Monsal Dale, and passes through the arches of a graceful railway viaduct. Simply stunning views.

Access: 3 miles north-west of Bakewell (on B6465).

Stable's Bar (Monsal Head Hotel)

Monsal Head. Tel (01629) 640250
www.monsalhead.com
Grid ref: 185715
Open: 11-11; 12-10.30 Sun.

Beer: Courage Directors; Marston's Pedigree; Whim Hartington Bitter; Monsal Bitter; Theakston's Best Bitter, Old Peculier; Timothy Taylor's Landlord. Plus a changing beer from the Abbeydale Brewery.

Food: Sizeable, tasty meals seved from 12 -9.30, ranging from regular snacks and children's meals through to unusual specials such as tiger prawn kebabs, and whole poached black bream. Eat in the

bar, or no-smoking Longstone Restaurant in the main hotel (open evenings Mon-Fri, and lunch/eve at weekends).

General: This popular hotel and nextdoor bar/pub was originally called the Bull's Head, then Station Hotel, since the main building served passengers brought up from the former railway station below. The horses were stabled in the building alongside, and this is now the comfortable one-room pub and contains a stone-flagged floor, large hearth and stove, and stalls named after horses (Samson, Blossom, Betty). It can get quite crowded at peak times, but with outside seating for 100 there's usually room in which to enjoy the decent food and wide selection of beers.

Royal Pub Signs

The Red Lion is believed to be one of the most common pub names in England (at least 500 at the last count). It was a badge of John o'Gaunt, Duke of Lancaster (1340-99), although in fact it is also part of the Royal Arms of Scotland. In the Peak District there are six Red Lions (see index). Other popular royal pub names include the Crown, which was often given to any inn located on royal land, and the King's Arms and the King's Head - although the face on the sign must have been changed quite frequently as monarchs came and went! The White Hart is still widespread, and refers to Richard II (1367-1400) whose coat of arms featured a swan and an antelope with a collar, which became a white stag on most signs. Another common name is the Royal Oak, commemorating the escape of Charles II in the Civil War by hiding in an oak tree.

MONYASH - Derbyshire

Formerly a thriving centre for rope making and lead mining, Monyash once had as many as five pubs and must have been a busy place. The village was granted a market charter in 1340 and had its own Barmote Court which adjudicated on local lead mining affairs. Later it became a strong base for the Quakers, and the 19th

Monyash – Over Haddon
Central / Eastern

century radical and Quaker, John Bright, often came to stay at nearby One Ash Grange. Today Monyash is especially popular with walkers and cyclists, situated on the Limestone Way and close to Lathkill Dale and the High Peak Trail.

Access: 4 miles south-west of Bakewell on B5055.

Bull's Head, Monyash

Bull's Head

Church Street. Tel (01629) 812372
Grid ref: 150660
Open: 12-3, 7-11; (11-11 Sat summer);
12-3, 7-11 (12-10.30 summer) Sun.
Beer: Tetley Bitter, Mild; Ind Coope Burton Ale, plus one guest beer.
Food: Home-cooked snacks and meals served lunchtime and evening until 9pm (9.30pm at weekends) with a changing specials board. Eat in main bar or separate dining rooms. Ravenous carnivores note Bully s Grill - steak, gammon, liver, sausage, black pudding, onion, tomato, mushroom and egg.
Accommodation: B&B - 2 doubles, 1 twin.
General: Large, handsome 17th century inn overlooking the village green, that for a (thankfully) short while was renamed The Hobbit . Tasty sizeable meals are popular with visitors, including walkers and families - benches at front, plus beer garden at rear with adjoining village playground. But it s also a popular local, with teams representing the pub at boules, netball, dominoes, pool, darts and football. Dogs allowed inside; live music vocalists every other Saturday.

The Peak National Park covers 555 square miles (1,438 sq kms)

NEWHAVEN - Derbyshire

Disparate hamlet astride the A515 (at junction with A5012), mid-way between Ashbourne and Buxton.

Jug and Glass

Ashbourne Road (A515), Newhaven/Hartington
Tel (01298) 84848
Grid ref: 157614
Open: 11-3, 6-11 (11-11 summer);
12-3, 6-10.30 (12-10.30 summer) Sun.
Beer: Bass, plus one guest beer.
Food: Well priced, hot and cold food served all day, including specials board (such as pork loin with peaches and honey; prawn and pollock prevençale) and numerous vegetarian choices (including mushroom goulash). No smoking throughout most of the pub.
General: Although originally an old ale house (c1800), the building has been completely renovated following a disastrous fire in 1995. Today the bright, new pub, sitting to the north of Newhaven near the Hartington turning (B5054), sells itself primarily on its good value meals. Forthcoming building work will include a disabled toilet, and there are plans for a beer garden to take advantage of the views over the hills towards Hartington, (the pub sits between the Tissington and High Peak Trails).

Hogshead: a 54-gallon cask

OVER HADDON - Derbyshire

Quiet and unspoilt, Over Haddon sits above one of the most delectable dales in the Peak District. Lathkill Dale (the pub is spelt with one 'l', incidentally) once echoed to the sound of lead mining, and indeed the pub used to be called the Miner's Arms; but now its mix of trout pools, ancient woodland and steep, limestone slopes makes it a haven for flowers, butterflies, birds and other wildlife. English Nature has an office in the village, with a visitor information barn next door, giving more details on the Derbyshire Dales Nature Reserve.
Access: 1 1/2 miles south of Bakewell (off B5055).

Lathkil Hotel

Over Haddon. Tel (01629) 812501
www.lathkil.co.uk
Grid ref: 207665
Open: 11.30-3, 7-11 (11-11 Sat summer);
12-3, 7-10.30 (12-10.30 summer) Sun.

Beer: Whim Hartington Bitter; Charles Wells Bombardier, plus two guest beers (such as Jennings Cumberland Ale; Marston's Pedigree; Kelham Island Easy Rider and beers from the Cottage Brewery).

Food: Lunchtime snacks and meals in bar and restaurant, evening (7-8.45) in restaurant only (part no-smoking). Menu may include lamb casserole and venison pie, plus sweets such as walnut flan, chocolate pear crunch, blackberry and apple crumble. Vegetarian menu; children's portions available; and carefully selected wines and malt whiskies.

Accommodation: B&B - 4 doubles (2 can be twin) all en-suite.

General: Attractive, whitewashed building in a peaceful position above open hillside, enjoying spectacular views over Lathkill Dale towards Youlgrave. Cosy bar with open fire (no children under 14) and light, spacious dining room, each with a wonderful White Peak panorama. Popular with walkers. Beer garden at side; dogs permitted indoors.

> *"Fill with mingled cream and amber,*
> *I will drain that glass again.*
> *Such hilarious visions clamber*
> *Through the chamber of my brain*
> *Quaintest thoughts and queerest fancies*
> *Come to life and fade away.*
> *What care I how time advances,*
> *I am drinking ale today."* Edgar Allen Poe

PILSLEY - Derbyshire

A mile from Chatsworth, this peaceful and preserved estate village of attractive, honey-coloured stone buildings retains a certain old fashioned charm. Edensor, another estate village situated in Chatsworth Park itself, tends to be more popular with visitors and once had eight pubs to accommodate their needs (but is now dry).

Access: 2½ miles north-east of Bakewell (off A619).

Devonshire Arms, Pilsley

Devonshire Arms

Pilsley. Tel (01246) 583258
Grid ref: 242712
Open: 11.30-2.30/3, 7-11; 12-2.30/3, 7-10.30 Sun.

Beer: Pilsley's Prime, when available (supplied by Bateman's).

Food: Traditional, home cooked food served every lunchtime, and Thurs-Sat 7.30-mid evening (including popular carvery). Dishes include roast beef angus, cod, and spring lamb. The function room is no-smoking.

Accommodation: B&B - 2 doubles, 1 twin.

General: This delightful 18th century pub is a long narrow building with four distinctive window gables and high chimneys. Its cosy main bar and dining room are comfortable and tastefully decorated, incorporating oak beams, thick set walls and open fires. Music every other Wednesday ('60s and country). Children and dogs in dining area only. A few tables outside.

POMEROY - Derbyshire

Situated on the A515 (Ashbourne-Buxton road), this hamlet is near the end of the High Peak Trail, and just over a mile from the village of Flagg.

Duke of York

Ashbourne Road (A515). Tel (01298) 83345
Grid ref: 119675
Open: 12-3, 6-11; 12-10.30 Sun.

Beer: Robinson's Best Bitter, Hartleys XB.

Food: Snacks and meals served lunchtime and evening up till 8.30, and all day on Sunday, in cosy main bar or large no-smoking dining room. The pub's emphasis on quality food is reflected in its changing specials board, which may include tuna steaks in orange sauce, swordfish, Lamb Henry in raspberry 'jus', and so on.

General: This former 15th century farmhouse became a popular coaching inn, and is a long, low building looking out over the limestone plateau towards Flagg and Monyash. There are beer gardens front and back, next to the large car park. Children in dining room only; no dogs. Oh yes, and beware the resident ghost, said to be that of local man William Pomeroy who several centuries ago was killed in a horse riding accident on the nearby road.

> *Flap-dragoning: an Elizabethan habit of adding an inflammable substance to the surface of liquor to give it an extra kick – the drink was called a flap dragon!*

ROBIN HOOD - Derbyshire

More of a location than a community, it's situated 1½ miles east of Baslow on the A619, by the B6050 Cutthorpe turning.

The real Robin Hood?

Look on the Ordnance Survey map and you'll see that the Robin Hood Inn really does stand at a place called Robin Hood (there's a similarly named farm next door). All over the eastern Peak District, references to the legendary hero abound: Robin Hood's Cave (Stanage Edge), Robin Hood's Stride (near Birchover), and Robin Hood's Cross (above Bradwell). Near Hathersage there's Robin Hood's Stoop, and of course in the village churchyard is a 10ft-long grave purported to be that of Little John. But isn't this just myth-making - we're in Derbyshire, not Nottinghamshire, aren't we? Perhaps, but don't forget that Robin Hood's supposed birthplace of Lockesley in South Yorkshire is not too far distant, and back in medieval times the old Sherwood Forest reached to the eastern edge of the Peak District. What was then a huge, impenetrable area must have harboured its fair share of outlaws and hideaways.

Robin Hood Inn

Robin Hood (near Baslow). Tel (01246) 583186
Grid ref: 280722
Open: 11-3, 6.30-11 (11-11 summer);
12-3, 6.30-10.30 (12-10.30 summer) Sun.
Beer: Mansfield Bitter, Dark Mild; Banks's Bitter; Marston's Pedigree.
Food: Standard range of snacks and meals served lunchtime and evenings 'till 8pm, including weekday senior citizens' specials.
Accommodation: B&B - 1 twin and 1 single.
General: Popular, modern pub on main road from Chesterfield, replacing the 17th century original which stood nearby. The back bar is known as the Hiker's Den, and is a favourite with walkers and climbers who flock to the area - Birchen Edge rises directly behind the pub, while across the road there's paths into Chatsworth estate. Children welcome until 9pm; small beer garden at side; dogs in Hiker's Den only.

ROWSLEY - Derbyshire

Sitting at the junction of the Wye and Derwent valleys, Rowsley was until quite recent times officially two separate places (Great and Little). The main square, on the Bakewell (western) bank of the Derwent, is dominated by the elegant façade of the Peacock Hotel. Its name reflects the family crest of the Duke of Rutland (the Manners family) of nearby Haddon Hall, and whose generosity over the centuries has provided the village with its school and church. Across the road is Caudwell's Mill, the last surviving water-powered flour mill in the country, and which still produces wholemeal flour, for sale to the public.
Access: 3 miles east of Bakewell on A6.

Grouse and Claret

Station Road (A6). Tel (01629) 733233
Grid ref: 257659
Open: 11-11; 12-10.30 Sun.
Beer: Mansfield Bitter; Banks's Bitter; Marston's Pedigree.
Food: Wide choice of set meals and snacks served 12-9 daily, including weekend carvery. Conservatory and most of main bar no-smoking.
Accommodation: B&B - 3 doubles, 2 single. Adjoining caravan park offers 29 pitches

(hard standing, with electric hook-ups), plus camping area, showers and toilets.

General: Large and popular family dining pub, with beer garden and extensive outside play area for children (including climbing frame). Inside is an open-plan bar and conservatory, plus an adults only tap room, dedicated wheelchair access and disabled toilets; no dogs allowed inside. Situated next to the new Peak Village retail shopping outlet. The pub was formerly called the Station Hotel, but with the demise of the railway it was renamed with the nearby River Derwent in mind - a grouse and claret is the name of a specialist dry fly used in trout fishing (see examples on wall display).

Peacock Hotel

Rowsley. Tel (01629) 733518
Grid ref: 256658
Open: 11-11; 12-10.30 Sun.
Beer: Ind Coope Burton Ale.
Food: Bar snacks served 12-2.30 only, or meals in plush no-smoking Garden Restaurant (12-2.30, 7-9.30). The latter's menu ranges from duck and lamb through to salmon and locally caught trout.
Accommodation: B&B - 16 en-suite rooms, including two 4-poster beds.
General: Built in 1652, this beautiful manor house was briefly the dower house to nearby Haddon Hall, and became a hotel in 1820. The ivy covered building includes a dark and atmospheric bar, with ornate woodwork and exposed beams, while the elegant restaurant contains period furniture and looks out on to the garden. Families and walkers welcome in bar; dogs in bedrooms only. The hotel is popular with fly fisherman who come to enjoy the Haddon Estate's seven mile stretch of the River Wye between Bakewell and Rowsley. The main catches are Rainbow trout, Brown trout and Grayling.

SHELDON - Derbyshire

Like Monyash, Youlgrave, Winster and so many other White Peak villages in this area, Sheldon's history is rooted in lead mining. Although the industry is no more and the village is now a quiet backwater,

you can still see some remains at nearby Magpie Mine (half a mile south of the village via footpaths). The former engine house, chimneys and even the more recent sheds and winding gear are preserved for posterity, and are a reminder what a tough and dangerous job it must have been deep underground.
Access: 2 miles west of Bakewell (off A6).

Cock and Pullet

Main Street. Tel (01629) 814292
Grid ref: 175687
Open: 11-11; 12-10.30 Sun.
Beer: Timothy Taylor's Landlord; Bass, plus one guest beer (such as Charles Wells Bombardier, Morland Old Speckled Hen etc).
Food: Tasty choice of snacks and meals served lunchtime and evening until 9pm, either in bar or adjoining no-smoking dining area. Specials include parsnip, leek and nut crumble, spinach and ricotta cannelloni, plus the usual Sunday roast lunch.
Accommodation: B&B - 2 double, 1 twin (all en-suite).
General: Opened as recently as 1995, this attractive village pub was once a barn, where dancing was held, and belonged to a former inn (the Devonshire Arms) that stood next door until its closure in 1971. The new pub is carefully furnished, and has a dark and cosy feel, with a central bar and adjoining, stone flagged pool room and dining area. Small patio seating area to the rear; families welcome, as are walkers. Wide doors, outside ramp and toilets designed for wheelchair users. Listen out every 15 minutes - the landlord's collection of 22 chiming clocks make quite a noise!

> *"Fermentation and Civilisation are inseparable"* John Cardi

STANTON IN PEAK - Derbyshire

Pleasantly isolated hilltop village overlooking Youlgrave and the lower Wye valley, Stanton in Peak was formerly the estate village of the Thornhill family who still live at Stanton Hall (private). From here it's a short walk on to Stanton Moor, a small and airy expanse of birch and springy heather, dotted with Bronze Age tumuli and the enigmatic Nine Ladies

Stanton in Peak – Taddington

Central / Eastern

Stone Circle. For suberb views of Haddon Hall and the Wye, head north-east out of the village on Pilhough Lane.

Access: 3 miles south-east of Bakewell (off B5056).

Flying Childers, Stanton in Peak

Flying Childers

Stanton-in-Peak. Tel (01629) 636333
Grid ref: 241643
Open: 12-2, 7-11 Tues-Fri; 12-3, 7-11 Sat; 12-3, 7-10.30 Sun.

Beer: Two changing cask beers, such as Adnams Bitter; Bateman's XB; Slaters Bitter, Whim Hartington Bitter, and so on.

Food: Cobs at lunchtime only.

General: Peaceful and unspoilt village local, converted from four cottages in the 18th century. It's named after a champion racehorse from the 1720s/30s, owned by the 4th Duke of Devonshire who retired the successful animal to his stud at Chatsworth when its racing career ended. This small and unpretentious, two-bar pub has real fires and is popular with locals and visitors (especially walkers). There is a small garden to the rear; children in top bar only; dogs allowed inside. The initials "WPT', carved into the stone above the entrance, stand for William Paul Thornhill, of Stanton Hall.

> *Cellar temperature: 54 °F (11 °C), the temperature at which purists say real ale (and red wine) should be served*

STARKHOLMES - Derbyshire

A quiet hillside village community above Matlock, reached by road from Matlock Green or Cromford Station (off the road to Riber Castle).

Access: 1 mile south of Matlock.

White Lion Inn

195 Starkholmes Road. Tel (01629) 582511
Grid ref: 302586
Open: 12-3, 5-11; 11-11 Sat; 12-10.30 Sun.

Beer: Marston's Pedigree; Home Bitter plus one guest beer (such as Timothy Taylor's Landlord; Whim Hartington Bitter).

Food: Lunchtime menu (12-2) offers light snacks and meals served in the no-smoking restaurant only. Appetising and highly original evening dishes, served (7-9) include roast quail salad and sauerkraut, Arbroath smokies, haggis, and pan-fried medallions of ostrich.

Accommodation: B&B - 2 doubles, 1 twin.

General: Handsome, 18th century coaching inn that was originally a farmhouse and cottages but has now become a long, knocked-through building. Apparently it was once called the Buddles Inn, after the locals who would 'buddle' (the old term for washing lead) in the barn next door. Inside it's comfortable and well-furnished, with low beamed ceilings and a small candlelit restaurant; while outside there's numerous picnic tables and a large car park. Children welcome if eating; dogs allowed away from the eating area only.

TADDINGTON - Derbyshire

In 1938 a short by-pass was built to re-route the busy A6 around this linear village, and ever since it's enjoyed a peaceful existence. At around 1,000 ft it sits atop the central limestone plateau of the White Peak, and nearby is the chambered cairn of Five Wells, the highest of its kind in the country.

Access: 5 miles east of Buxton on A6.

Queen's Arms

Main Street. Tel (01298) 85245
Grid ref: 147711
Open: 12-3, 7(5.30 Fri)-11; 12-3, 7-10.30 Sun.

Beer: Bass; Greene King IPA, plus one guest beer (previously Black Sheep Best Bitter, beers from the Badger Brewery etc).

Food: Wide-ranging menu with specials board served lunchtime and evening (7-9). Thursday's speciality is steak (rump, gammon, pork or turkey escalope), while the fish and chip tea each Friday (5.30-6.30) features haddock in beer batter. Try the genuinely home-made quiches, flans, soups, etc, in either the main bar, conservatory or parlour (no-smoking).

General: Opened in 1736 as the Miner's Arms when lead-mining was the main employer, this welcoming village pub was also the stopping-off point for passing stagecoaches when the London Road – the modern A6 – formed the main street. The high, main room wraps around the central bar, with a cosy, boxed window area (the conservatory) and a separate public bar (the parlour). The pub also served as a temporary morgue for a while, but now the visitors depart alive and extremely well-fed. Families and children welcome; a couple of outside picnic tables to rear; occasional live music.

> *You are now allowed 20 minutes 'drinking-up' time at the end of a pub's normal opening hours - or 30 minutes if you have bought the drink as part of a sit-down meal.*

Waterloo Hotel

Taddington. Tel (01298) 85230
Grid ref: 134714
Open: 12-3, 7-11; 12-3, 7-10.30 Sun.
Beer: Robinson's Best Bitter, plus Robinson's seasonal beer (such as Stockport's Arches).
Food: Traditional range of sandwiches and main meals served lunchtime and evening until 9pm. Thursday is pie night (steak, salmon and broccoli, chicken and mushroom, etc), Friday is fish, and Saturday it's steak, when there's well-priced deals on main course and sweets. Served in bar or small no-smoking dining room.
Accommodation: B&B - 3 double, 1 twin, en-suite.
General: Situated just under 1/2 mile west of Taddington village on the A6, this former farm is now a large, bright building with an open-plan bar and comfy seats arranged around an open fire. At the far end is a spacious function room that is hired out to private groups ('142 dancing, 238 seated' stipulates an official sign!). Families welcome, as are walkers – the pub is actually on the Limestone Way long distance footpath. There's a beer garden at the rear. No dogs inside.

TANSLEY - Derbyshire

Located one mile east of Matlock (on A615). The ruined mills below Tansley Knoll and at nearby Lumsdale, are testimony to the area's former activities.

Royal Oak

Nottingham Road (A615). Tel (01629) 57412
Grid ref: 323595
Open: 12-3, 7-11; 12-3, 7-10.30 Sun.
Beer: Kimberley Best Bitter, plus seasonal beers from Kimberley.
Food: Hot and cold food served each lunchtime and Thurs-Sun evenings until 9.15pm, in bar area or newly opened no-smoking room. The changing blackboard choices include pies, pasta, fish and the whopping 'Oak Grill'.
General: A bright, cheerful roadside pub in a former 18th century farm building. It contains one long open main bar, a no-smoking room and upstairs pool room. Pub teams also participate in skittles, darts and the Barmote quiz league. Children are welcome, there is an outside play area (climbing frame, swings) on a grassy strip by the picnic tables at rear. Dogs allowed inside.

Tavern at Tansley

Nottingham Road (A615). Tel (01629) 57735
Grid ref: 324596
Open: 12-3, 6-11; 12-10.30 Sun.
Beer: Marston's Pedigree; Tetley Bitter; Morland Old Speckled Hen.
Food: Very popular eating establishment, with a wide range of meals and snacks served each lunchtime and evening ('till 8.45pm Mon/Tues, and 9.30pm Wed-Sun). In addition to the set menu and specials (á la carte only on Fri/Sat), there are regular themed meals, such as fish and vegetarian night on Tues, 'Crazy Steak Night' each Wed, and sizzle and griddle night on Thurs. Eat in the bar or 40-seat no-smoking restaurant; booking is advisable for weekends.
Accommodation: B&B - 3 en-suite double rooms.
General: Busy, lively pub catering for all ages, with a children's adventure playground and bouncy castle outside, plus

adults-only garden at rear. No dogs. Children welcome inside if eating. Originally the building used to be a farm and milking parlour, and until quite recently the pub was called the George and Dragon.

TIDESWELL - Derbyshire

Foremost among Tideswell's attractions is the parish church of St John the Baptist, popularly known as the 'Cathedral of the Peak', which dates from the 14th century. The distinctive Perpendicular-style tower was added much later, and the churchyard contains a number of interesting items including an ancient cross and a sundial. There is also the grave of the so-called 'Minstrel of the Peak', William Newton. Well-dressing takes place during the Wakes Week in June, and with plenty of shops and numerous lanes and passageways there's plenty to explore.

Access: 5 miles east of Buxton (off A623).

Anchor Inn

Four Lanes End (on A623 junction beyond the north-eastern end of village). Tel (01298) 871371
Grid ref: 159763
Open: 12-2.30, 5-11; 12-2.30, 5-10.30 Sun.
Beer: Robinson's Best Bitter, with occasional Robinson's seasonal beer.
Food: Traditional pub food served lunchtime and evening, until 9pm. Specialises in char-grill (steaks, gammon, etc) and curries cooked to order.
General: Despite its whitewashed appearance the wooden-panelled interior gives this former farmstead a dark and enclosed feeling. There are two bars (dogs in taproom only), and a restaurant at the rear. Families welcome. Picnic tables at front, but what were once horse-drawn coaches, leaving the busy Nottingham-Manchester turnpike have been replaced by faster and certainly louder traffic.

George Hotel

Commercial Road. Tel (01298) 871382
Grid ref: 153758
Open: 10.30-3, 7-11; 12-3, 7-10.30 Sun.
Beer: Kimberley Best Bitter, plus a Kimberley seasonal beer.
Food: Varied menu, including venison, gammon and guinea fowl, plus daily specials board. Meals seved in either bar area or no-smoking restaurant, 12-2, 7-9, but not Sunday night.
Accommodation: B&B - 4 rooms, 2 en-suite (3 doubles – including one 4-poster, and 1 triple).
General: Built in 1730, this attractive coaching inn next to the church has a series of comfortable, open rooms, including a pool room and dining area, plus real fires in winter. There's a small garden at the rear, and live music (60s/70s) tales place every Friday. Children and dogs welcome.

George Hotel, Tideswell

Horse and Jockey

Queen Street. Tel (01298) 871597
Grid ref: 153756
Open: 10.30-3, 7-11; 12-3, 7-10.30 Sun.
Beer: John Smith's Bitter; Tetley Bitter, plus one guest such as Morland Old Speckled Hen.
Food: Usual range of pub food served lunchtime and evening, until 9pm. Includes dishes such as seafood pancake, chicken and leek in stilton sauce, salmon and asparagus; plus traditional Sunday roast.
General: Small and unassuming two bar-pub, sitting amid terraced cottages on the main road out of the southern end of the village towards Miller's Dale. Live music monthly, plus tap room features an upright piano. Outside seating by pavement at front, plus small area at rear. Children welcome; dogs in tap room only.

Star Inn

High Street. Tel (01298) 872397
Grid ref: 153758
Open: 5 (11 Sat)-11; 12-10.30 Sun.
Beer: Tetley Bitter; Black Sheep Best Bitter,

plus one guest beer (e.g. Everards Tiger).
Food: Hot and cold snacks served 'till 9/9.30 in the evening, all day at weekends, and include 'Star Super Sandwiches' and toasted filled baguettes. Eat in either of the bars, or separate dining room.
General: Rather tucked away on a side road (in fact the original high street) heading north out of the village, this unpretentious locals' pub comprises three tiny bars and a side room. The new owners are gradually refurbishing the interior, but the original, unspoilt feel of the place remains. There are a couple of roadside benches but no garden; children, dogs, and all-comers welcome.

WARDLOW MIRES - Derbyshire

A rather lonely location just to the south of the village of Wardlow in the high central limestone plateau, and which although not particularly remote can feel bleak and isolated in bad weather. Here, in 1815, the last public gibbeting in Derbyshire took place, when a 21 year old man was found guilty of murdering Hannah Oliver, tollkeeper at Wardlow Mires. A short walk along nearby Cressbrook Dale is the distinctively shaped Peter's Stone.
Access: 5 miles north-west of Bakewell (junction of A623/B6465).

Three Stags Heads

Wardlow Mires (A623). Tel (01298) 872268
Grid ref: 182756
Open: 7-11 Fri only; 11-11 Sat and Bank Holidays; 12-10.30 Sun.
Beer: Abbeydale Absolution, Matins, Black Lurcher, and Broadstone Charter Bitter.
Food: Traditional, freshly-prepared dishes served on home-made crockery. Includes likes of pies, liver and onion, a vegetarian option, plus game in season (hare, grouse, pigeon, pheasant, rabbit). Served 12-3, 7-9.30. Small dining room available.
General: As you lift the latch, and walk into this small unpretentious pub, you'll take an immediate liking, or head straight back out again. The two small rooms (plus a tiny dining room) are simple and unfussy, with wooden benches and settles, scrubbed wooden tables and a stone-flagged floor,

plus attractive open ranges that make it especially cosy in the winter. This is a pub for conversation, interrupted only by lively folk sessions on Saturday nights. Amongst the ever-present dogs is the landlord's handsome Black Lurcher - the potent beer of that name is specially brewed for the pub. The home-made pottery is for sale. Small seating area at front.

WENSLEY - Derbyshire

Hillside village between Darley Bridge and Winster overlooking the Derwent valley.
Access: 2 miles west of Matlock on B5057.

Red Lion

Main Road. Tel (01629) 732578
Grid ref: 263612
Open: 11-11; 12-10.30 Sun.
Beer: Bottled beer only.
Food: Home-baked cobs, such as ham and (home-grown) beetroot, cheese and onion, etc, plus soups and light snacks to order. The owners also make their own milkshakes, including the 'Milliguin' which features half a pint of milk and half a pint of Guinness.
General: A fascinating old place that has refused to yield to the world of mod cons – don't expect plush seating, fruit machines or hand driers. Instead, the two basic bars are adorned with a fascinating array of pub and brewery memorabilia of the 1950s-70s, including an odd photo of the landlady as a baby inside a boot. The pub's been in the family since 1949, when the present landlord helped his mother run it while the father farmed. No smoking throughout the pub; no dogs; seating outside (summer only).

WINSTER - Derbyshire

A traditional and very attractive White Peak village that still retains its late 17th century arched Market House (acquired by the National Trust in 1906, its first property in Derbyshire). When the local lead mining industry was in full swing Winster had as many as 20 inns and alehouses, including the Georgian Winster Hall on the main street (now a private house). Today it's down to just two. However traditions are kept alive, by amongst others, the Winster Morris Men, a troupe famous throughout the Peak District. During the annual village carnival they perform their so-called 'Winster Gallop' outside the Old Bowling Green. **Access:** 3 miles west of Matlock on B5057.

The Old Market Hall, Winster

Miners Standard

Bank Top (on B5056, just outside the top end of the village). Tel (01629) 650279.
Grid ref: 237603
Open: 12-4, 6.30-11; 12-4, 6.30-10.30 Sun.
Beer: Marston's Pedigree; Bass; Boddingtons Bitter, plus one seasonal winter beer.
Food: Tasty range of snacks and meals served lunchtime and evenings until 9pm in bar, family room or no-smoking dining room. Large portions and well-priced, with home-made pies a speciality: steak, ham and stilton, cheese and onion, etc, plus seasonal game pies.
Accommodation: Field for tents and caravans at rear (outside toilets).
General: This large, comfortable old pub dates from as far back as 1653, and is named after the so-called 'standard dish' once used by lead miners to measure their ore (see the example in the pub itself). Off the main bar is a cosy snug at the rear, plus a newer family/games room (children welcome), and a sizeable dining room overlooking the beer garden. Popular with walkers; dogs permitted inside. The initials EP EP FP above the main entrance refer to the original owners (Edward Parker, his wife Elizabeth and their son Francis), although an alternative version is: 'Every person entering pays for a pint'!

> *"Beer is living proof that God loves us and wants us to be happy."* Benjamin Franklin

Old Bowling Green

East Bank. Tel (01629) 650219
Grid ref: 243604
www.bowlinggreen.co.uk
Open: 6 (11 Sat)-11; 12-10.30 Sun.
Beer: Up to four beers including Black Sheep Best Bitter; Tetley Bitter; Whim Hartington Bitter etc. Also look out for the impressive range of malt whiskies.
Food: Range of traditional dishes prepared on the premises, including Chicken Hartington and Mediterranian lamb casserole, served every evening from 6-9, and weekends 12-2, throughout the pub (large no-smoking area).
General: Dating from the 14th century, but considerably refurbished, this attractive village local has a large, comfortable lounge bar and pleasant conservatory. Outside seating at front and rear, where there is also a floodlit boules pitch. Children are allowed inside if eating (no later than 8pm). No dogs. Walkers welcome. The faces depicted on one side of the pub sign are late relatives and friends of the landlord.

> *"But I'm not so think as you drunk I am."* J C Squire

YOULGRAVE - Derbyshire

Like Winster this very pleasant, linear village still maintains a strong resident community, with shops, a post office, garage and health centre, plus in Youlgrave's case three inviting pubs. The place is known locally as "Pommy" (believed to be a historical reference to the noise made by its silver band), and its name has been spelt in numerous ways - 'Youlgreave' is favoured by the Ordnance Survey, but the village road sign reflects the local' preference for 'Youlgrave'. The village is well-known for its well-dressings which occur in late June when five wells are ritually blessed. This is also a very popular area for walkers, with the attractions of nearby Bradford Dale and Lathkill Dale, as well as the Limestone Way and White Peak Way. In the centre of Youlgrave is a youth hostel, housed in the handsome former village Co-op stores.
Access: 3 miles south-east of Bakewell (off A6).

Bull's Head

Fountain Square. Tel (01629) 636307
Grid ref: 211643
Open: 11.30-3, 6.30-11; 12-3, 7-10.30 Sun.

Beer: Marston's Bitter, Pedigree; Banks's Bitter.

Food: Lunchtime and evening meals served 'till 8.45pm in bars or no-smoking dining room. Full range of snacks and hot meals, including Sunday roast, plus home-made specials or à la carte menu.

Accommodation: B&B - 4 rooms (2 doubles, 2 twin) and en-suite ground floor flat.

General: Large and attractive old pub in centre of village, situated next to youth hostel and shops. Three rooms, plus small no-smoking restaurant, with a few pavement seats outside front and in courtyard. Snooker/pool room upstairs. Children welcome; dogs allowed inside (not restaurant). NB. The author's local; he will be pleased to buy anyone a pint of Pedigree, if they flourish a copy of this guide.

Farmyard Inn

Main Street. Tel (01629) 636221
Grid ref: 208643
Open: 11.30-3, 7-11; 12-3, 7-10.30 Sun.

Beer: Bass; Greene King IPA.

Food: Standard but popular bar food served lunchtime and evening (until 8-8.30), plus full à la carte menu (grills, steaks, fish – including halibut and sea bass) in no-smoking, upstairs Triton Restaurant (Tue-Sat, 7-9).

Accommodation: B&B - 3 en-suite chalet rooms (2 double, 1 twin).

General: Originally a 300 year old, farm-house, the building has been used as a pub since 1829, and still retains an authentic air. The long, low and snug bar has an inviting open fire at the far end, with a small pool room next door and air-conditioned restaurant upstairs (it's named after a classic motorbike, restored by one of the owners and now on display, in case you're wondering). No children after 9pm; dogs are not allowed inside during eating times. Small beer garden by car park.

Stout: rich and full-bodied dark ale brewed with black malt.

George Hotel, Youlgrave

George Hotel

Church Street. Tel (01629) 636292
Grid ref: 213644
Open: 11-11; 12-10.30 Sun.

Beer: John Smith's Bitter; plus two guests (such as Theakston's Mild; Brakspear Bee Sting; Jennings Snecklifter).

Food: Wide range of home-cooked dishes (and generous portions, too!) prepared on premises, many including locally sourced game: venison, port and redcurrant pie, savoury braised pheasant in orange, etc. Served lunchtime and evening, Mon-Fri ('till 9pm), and all day at weekends.

Accommodation: B&B - 3 double rooms (2 en-suite).

General: Traditional 17th century village local, opposite the imposing All Saints Church. The light, high-ceiling pub has three distinct bars, including a tap room and cosy back room, and a refreshing absence of piped music or one-armed bandits. But which monarch the pub is named after is unclear – hence four King Georges are depicted on the sign outside! Families welcome; dogs in tap room only; some roadside seating out the front.

A sad farewell – the lost pubs

Of course like any privately run business new public houses open or are taken over all the time, just as others close down and disappear. This has always happened, but recent research by the Campaign for Real Ale (CAMRA) has shown that the rate of closures is speeding up and across the country as many as 20 pubs are closing each month.

In the Central-East area of the Peak District the list of former pubs is considerable, but it must be remembered that a couple of hundred years ago, in the heyday of Derbyshire's lead-mining industry, many of what now appear to be sleepy little hamlets and villages were busy communities that contained numerous pubs and ale houses. At one time **Winster** had more than 20 (today it has two), including the Angel, Shoulder of Mutton and the Crown, and on the B5056 just north of the village the Piper Inn, which fell derelict in the 1930s. Records show that in 1765 there were as many as 13 inns in **Bakewell**, but by 1809 only nine. Among those now gone are the Anchor (knocked into the Wheatsheaf), the White Horse Inn (demolished to make way for the Rutland Arms), the King's Arms (previously the Crown Inn, on Buxton Road), Britain's Pride (which became Skidmores greengrocers), the Nag's Head and the Royal Oak Inn.

Apparently **Bonsall** once sported the Britannia, Miner's Standard, Queens Head, Fountain Inn and New Inn, while the Pig o'Lead Inn (formerly the Via Gellia Inn) at the junction with nearby Via Gellia was closed in 1995 to be made into a private home. At one time the tiny Chatsworth estate village of **Edensor** had as many as eight pubs or ale outlets, partly to cater for the tourist traffic; while the Snake and Crown could once be found at the other Chatsworth village of **Pilsley**. At **Youlgrave** the Thornhill Arms (opposite the church, near the George Hotel) is now a private residence, and so is the Bateman Arms in **Middleton-by-Youlgrave**, which was named after the famous Victorian antiquarian who lived locally. Just along from here is the hamlet of **Gratton**, at the head of peaceful Bradford Dale. Back in 1970s passers by were confused by a sign for the non existent Black Dog public house. It turned out to be a temporary affair created for the set of 'The Virgin and the Gypsy', a film of D H Lawrence's book that was shot in the area.

Elsewhere, **Miller's Dale** once had the Railway, which changed its name to the Dale and closed in the mid 1970s; Monyash's five former pubs included the Golden Lion and Bay Horse; and at **Pikehall** the Pikeham Inne is now Pikehall Farm. **Sheldon's** Devonshire Arms closed in 1971, but happily the old barn next door was converted into the Cock and Pullet in 1995. On Commerical Road in the centre of **Tideswell** you could once find the Bull's Head and King's Head, the latter now replaced with the Co-op supermarket. In **Wensley** the Crown closed as recently as 1997, and although only the Queen's Arms is left in **Taddington** former pubs included the Bull's Head, George Inn, Star Inn and Travellers Rest.

Traditional pub games

For many pub-goers the insidious spread of brightly-flashing fruit machines and video games, piped 'wallpaper' music and raucous karaoke evenings have ruined the atmosphere and appearance of some fine old establishments. Thankfully there are still plenty of pubs across the Peak District where you can sit and enjoy a quiet conversation, rather than feel you have gate-crashed a nightclub or entered a casino. Most of them are featured in the pages of this book, and what's more some still retain a few traditional pub games that have been enjoyed in the inns and taverns of this country for hundreds of years.

Many if not most pubs have their own teams for various sports and activities. Darts and pool are two of the most common, plus there are numerous pub quiz leagues (the author represents his local in one such). There are pubs in this book who also have their own football, cricket and netball teams, and some have been developing their own outdoors boules pitches where eagerly-fought league matches routinely take place - visit the **Malt Shovel** (Wirksworth Moor), **Farmyard Inn** (Youlgrave), **Rising Sun** (Middleton by Wirksworth) and the **Old Bowling Green** (Winster) to find out more about this entertaining French import. The indoors pursuit of bar billiards, which is thought to have originated from the popular 19th century pub game bagatelle, is still quite popular in southern England, but in the Peak District few tables remain. The **Little John Hotel** in Hathersage still has one, and a fine example can still be seen at the **Lathkil Hotel** at Over Haddon. Another traditional English pub game that has sadly almost died out in the Peak District is skittles, or nine pins, the forerunner of 10-pin bowling, where wooden balls are rolled down a lane to knock over skittles. The **Bentley Brook Inn** at Fenny Bentley still has two outdoor alleys, and skittles also take place at the **Royal Oak** (Tansley) and the **Red Lion** (Kniveton). However, a miniature version of this game called bar or table skittles can still be found at a few pubs, such as the **Duke William** at Matlock and the **Plough Inn** at Flagg (which also has a bar billiards table).

You can still find games of dominoes played in the tap room of some local Peak pubs, such as the **George Hotel**, Youlgrave. It's a game that hasn't changed that much since the Chinese first played it in the 14th century (except they probably weren't sitting around with a pint and a roll-up). The game arrived in Britain in the late 18th century from France, possibly via French prisoners of war, and the word 'domino' is French for a black and white hood worn by priests in winter.

Did you know that cribbage is the only card game that can legally be played for money in English pubs? Cribbage, or crib, has its roots in a Tudor game called 'Noddy', and was made famous by the 17th century poet and gambler Sir John Suckling who managed to cheat much of England's wealthy aristocracy out of their money by distributing packs of marked cards then beating them at cribbage. Visit the **King's Head** in Bonsall to see an original gaming table.

Part Two: Northern Area

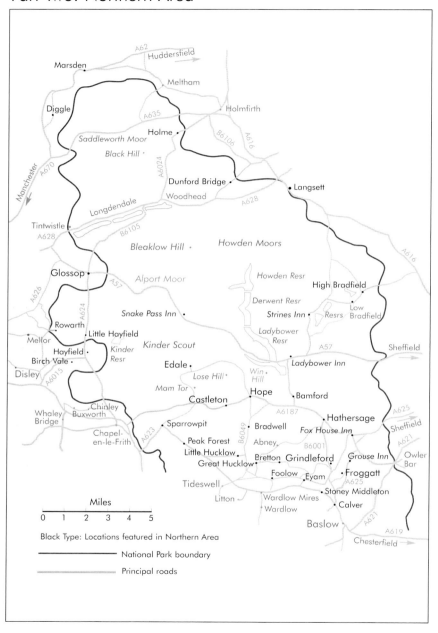

Miles

0   1   2   3   4   5

Black Type: Locations featured in Northern Area

━━━━━━━━━━ National Park boundary

━━━━━━━━━━ Principal roads

BAMFORD - Derbyshire

Bamford sits above the River Derwent in the gap between the Hope Valley and Ladybower Reservoir - its name is thought to mean 'ford with a tree trunk (or beam)'. The modern settlement developed around a water-powered cotton mill, opened in 1782, and a century later was further enhanced with the coming of the Sheffield railway. The latter included a valley branch line to supply quarried stone for the building of the Howden and Derwent dams, which were completed in the early 1900s. **Access:** 2 miles north-west of Hathersage (on A6013).

Anglers Rest

Taggs Knoll. Tel (01433) 651424
Grid ref: 208837
Open: 12-3, 6-11 Mon-Fri; 11-11 Sat; 12-10.30 Sun.
Beer: Mansfield Bitter; Marston's Pedigree; Banks's Bitter.
Food: Served 12-2.30, 6-9. Set menu and changing specials board, the latter including halibut steak, Tiger prawn salad and vegetarian options.
General: Located just off the main street at the top of the village (opposite the Bamford Institute), this long and solid-looking pub was built in 1876, and exudes a dark and cosy feel. At one end is the small main bar, with a split-level dining area occupying the rest of the narrow building. Disabled toilet by doorway to car park, at far end of dining room. Families welcome; small outdoor seating area at rear. Live music every 1-2 months.

Derwent Hotel

Main Road. Tel (01433) 651395
Grid ref: 207835
Open: 11-11; 12-10.30 Sun.
Beer: Stones; John Smith's Bitter plus one guest beer (Fuller's London Pride; Marston's Pedigree, etc.)
Food: Served 12-2.30, 6-9 (Mon), all day 'till 9pm (Sun). Choose from an extensive menu, including specials (rack of lamb, trio of fish), with steak night each Friday and a Sunday and Bank Holiday carvery. You can eat throughout the pub, although there's one main, no-smoking dining room.

Accommodation: 12 rooms (8 en-suite), with 5 doubles, 3 twins, 2 family rooms and 2 singles.
General: Quaint cottage pub this isn't, rather it's a high, twin-gabled building containing four open rooms (including a pool room) with high ceilings and lots of light. Children welcome (not at the bar); garden at rear, and some seats out front and side; dogs in tap room only. Live music normally every Mon and Fri - everything from singers and bands to discos and cabarets, and at weekends it can get quite lively. A courtesy bus operates for customers staying nearby.

Rising Sun

Castleton Road (A6187). Thornhill Moor.
Tel (01433) 651323
www.the-rising-sun.org
Grid ref: 196828
Open: 11-11; 12-10.30 Sun.
Beer: Bass; Morland Old Speckled Hen.
Food: Served in main bar 12-3 (3.30 Sun), 6.30-10 (7-9 Sun), the front part of which is no-smoking. Choice of sandwhiches and bar food (shepherd's pie, chicken balti, eggs Benedict) or main courses such as fresh whole lemon sole, fillet steak stuffed with stilton, slow-roasted belly pork with Hoisin sauce and noodles.
Accommodation: B&B - 12 en-suite rooms.
General: This attractive, mock-Tudor fronted hotel was built in 1795, at which time it was a small roadside tavern just called the Sun. It stood by a toll gate on what is now the main road along the Hope Valley, a mile south-west of Bamford in the parish of Thornhill. Inside there is one spacious bar, plush and comortable, with a secluded lawned garden to the rear with views of the hills. Well-behaved children welcome; ditto dogs.

> *"Wine comes in at the mouth*
> *And love comes in at the eye,*
> *That's all that we know for truth*
> *Before we grow old and die.*
> *I lift the glass to my mouth,*
> *I look at you and sigh."*
> William Butler Yeats

North

Yorkshire Bridge Inn

Bamford (on A6013). Tel (01433) 651361
www.yorkshire-bridge.co.uk
Grid ref: 196828
Open: 11-11; 12-10.30 Sun.

Beer: Theakston's Best Bitter, Old Peculier, Bass; Stones Bitter.

Food: Served lunchtime and evening ('till 9pm) and all-day Sunday, the menu offers sandwiches and salad platters through to a variety of main meals. The specials board includes crispy duck, goats cheese, red pesto and tomato quiche, and pot-roasted lamb. There are four separate eating rooms, including a light and airy conservatory.

Accommodation: Extensive accommodation block, offering 14 en-suite bedrooms (9 double, 2 double/twin, 2 family, 1 four poster).

General: Named after a nearby pack-horse bridge, which was once the only crossing point of the River Derwent for travellers from Yorkshire to Derbyshire (the Yorkshire border is only 3 miles away). This large and bustling pub located one mile north of Bamford does a good trade from anglers, as well as passing tourists, who come to fish the nearby reservoirs. Children welcome (outside play area and seating at front and back); dogs allowed inside after food hours; fully wheelchair-friendly, with ramps and disabled toilet.

BIRCH VALE - Derbyshire

A small, linear community in the Sett Valley mid-way between Hayfield and New Mills.

Sycamore Inn

Sycamore Road. Tel (01663) 742715/747568
www.sycamoreinn.co.uk
Grid ref: 011868
Open: 11-11; 12-10.30 Sun.

Beer: Marston's Pedigree; John Smith's Bitter; Robinson's Best Bitter.

Food: Wide range of food served all day 'till 10pm. Mon-Sat lunchtime menu up to 4/5pm and includes warm baguettes, salads and light snacks, while the evening menu includes specials such as salmon Dieppe, hot and spicy beef stir fry, plus vegetarian and children's options. Eat in bar or large dining room (includes a no-smoking area).

Accommodation: 6 en-suite B&B rooms.

General: Located off a lane on northern side of the Sett Valley - leave A6015 in Birch Vale, for road signposted Thornsett. Large and roomy hillside building (two storeys at the front, four at the rear!), now plush and comfortable after considerable renovation. It's very popular with groups and families, and apart from the usual outside seating there's a children's pets corner and adventure playground by the car park below. Dogs allowed inside.

Waltzing Weasel

New Mills Road (A6015). Tel (01633) 743402
www.w-weasel.co.uk
Grid ref: 014866
Open: 12-3, 5.30-11; 12-3, 5.30 -10.30 Sun.

Beer: Marston's Bitter; Timothy Taylor's Landlord.

Food: Superior eating pub with original and mouth-watering menu, specialities include vegetarian (roasted fennel, tarte provençale, vegetable crepe), Italian (Abacchio alla Romana, home-made pizzas) and 'peasant casseroles or stew cooking' (Greek stifado, Italian beef, Moroccan vegetable, Middle Eastern tagine). Served in bar from 12-2, 7-9.30 (9pm Sun) and elegant no-smoking restaurant 7-9 (8.30pm Sun).

Accommodation: 8 en-suite rooms (1 single, 2 twin, 5 double)

General: A traditional inn for over 200 years (it used to be called the Birch Hall Inn until the 1960s), this thoughtfully decorated, open-plan pub is comfortable and relaxed with no fruit machines or jukeboxes - even mobile phones are banned. Children over 9 are welcome - in restaurant only. Dogs allowed inside; plus there's a small area of outside patio seating with views across the Sett Valley to Kinder Scout.

BRADFIELD - South Yorkshire

Bradfield lies at the far north-eastern edge of the Peak National Park, and its rural hillside location belies its proximity to Sheffield. There are three parts (Low Bradfield, Bradfield and High Bradfield), and the Old Horns Inn is at the top of the hill at, rather inevitably, High Bradfield. Also make sure to visit the nearby Church of St Nicholas, which has the largest parish in England, and sports a curious 18th century Watch House at the entrance to the churchyard that was built to keep an eye out for nocturnal body-snatchers!

Access: 5 miles north-west of Sheffield.

Old Horns Inn

High Bradfield. Tel (0114) 2851207
Grid ref: 267924
Open: 12-4, 5.30-11 Mon, Tues and Thurs;
11-11 Wed, Fri & Sat; 12-10.30 Sun.

Beer: Stones Bitter; John Smith's Magnet, Theakston's Best Bitter; Courage Directors, plus one guest beer.

Food: Wide-ranging blackboard menu, including sandwiches and light snacks through to a changing list of hot meals. Unusual selections include wild rice and spinach roast, lemon sole, and honey roast duck, and there are regular themed food nights (Indian, Caribbean, Scottish, etc). Served throughout the bar (one part no-smoking) 12-3, 5.30-9 daily.

General: Solid and handsome old stone building overlooking a wide valley dotted with small reservoirs and farmsteads. There are tremendous views from the scattering of picnic tables next to the cordoned-off children's play area. Inside, there's one comfortable, open-plan bar that wraps around the pub, including a no-smoking area, and a restaurant is to be built soon. There are no restrictions on families, or dogs, and the pub also has a disabled toilet (level entrance at the front, steps from the car park at the rear).

BRADWELL - Derbyshire

'Bradder' is a large village in the Hope valley near Castleton, that despite its quiet, pleasant back streets is probably better known for its cement works and delicious ice cream. There was a Roman presence here, as a small fort known as Navio was located at nearby Brough in a bend of the River Noe. In 1806 miners discovered Bagshawe Cavern, which can be visited by organised caving trips (you do get wet and muddy, but it is well worth it).

Access: Two miles south-east of Castleton on B6049.

Olde Bowling Green

Smalldale. Tel (01433) 620450
Grid ref: 172816
Open: 11-11; 12-10.30 Sun.

Beer: Stones Bitter; Bass, plus one guest beer (such as Fuller's London Pride; Black Sheep Best Bitter; Timothy Taylor's Landlord).

Food: Set menu and specials served every lunchtime 'till 9pm. Wide range of cold snacks and hot meals, from pies and steaks to fish and pastas, served in large dining area (part no-smoking).

Accommodation: B&B - 6 en-suite rooms (1 twin, 5 double, including a 4-poster).

General: Large and pleasantly sprawling 16th century building in the Smalldale area of Bradwell (north-west of the centre). Dark and comfortable albeit modernised interior – one room with a pool table, the other seating and open fire. Good views over the Hope valley from the patio seating and large lawned garden. Walkers and familes welcome; dogs in garden only.

BRETTON - Derbyshire

An exposed and isolated location at a height of over 1,200 feet, on a bare ridge north of Foolow and Eyam. There's little here apart from the pub, a farm and a youth hostel. Depending on the time of year and prevailing weather, you can either laze on the grass and enjoy the terrific views, or do battle against the wind as you make for the pub door.

Access: Six miles north of Bakewell (off A623).

Barrel Inn, Bretton

Bretton – Castleton

North

Barrel Inn

Bretton. Tel (01433) 630856

Grid ref: 201779

Open: 11-3, 6 -11; 11-11 Sat; 12-10.30 Sun.

Beer: Tetley Bitter; Marston's Pedigree, and two guest beers (such as Greene King Abbot Ale; Adnams Broadside, etc).

Food: Snacks and meals served lunchtime and evening ('till 9.30). Freshly prepared specials include shank of lamb braised with red wine and thyme, Red Snapper, breast of duck, lamb pasander.

Accommodation: 1 en-suite family room (sleeps up to four).

General: On a clear day Derbyshire's highest pub (1,250 feet above sea level) gives arguably the finest view in the White Peak. Originally a farmhouse, the building is over 400 years old. The oak beamed bar is supplemented by a few outside tables, or take your drink across the lane to the benches at the top of the hillside opposite. Irish folk music in the form of a ceilidh, every Wednesday evening; no children after 8pm; dogs allowed inside, and tie up for horses to the side of the pub.

CALVER - Derbyshire

Pronounced 'Carver', most of this quiet village sits back from the busy crossroads known as Calver Sough. (A sough is the term for a drainage tunnel for lead mines.) Adjacent to the River Derwent is Calver Mill, a former water-powered cotton mill, built in 1785 and closed in the 1920s. Due to its huge, rather forbidding appearance it was used as a set for the 1970s TV series 'Colditz'! It has recently been transformed into private luxury accommodation.

Access: Four miles north-east of Bakewell (A623/B6001).

Bridge Inn

Calver Bridge. Tel (01433) 630415

Grid ref: 247745

Open: 11.30-3, 5.30-11; 12-3.30, 7-10.30 (Sun).

Beer: Kimberley Best Bitter, Classic, plus a Kimberley seasonal beer.

Food: Traditional and popular range of hot and cold food served every lunchtime, and 6.30-8.30 Tues-Sat (plus 7-8 on summer Sundays). Specials board includes Cajun chicken, rump steak, and cod and prawn crumble. The top end of one bar is no-smoking.

General: Small and friendly two bar pub next to the historic crossing of the River Derwent between Calver and Curbar. Originally a ford, then a wooden bridge, the centuries-old stone bridge was finally superseded by an ugly modern crossing in 1974. You can scrutinise them both from the ample garden seating on the river's edge. Comfortable and cosy inside, with open fires, look out for the landlord's collection of antique fire-fighting equipment. Walkers welcome; children inside, if eating; dogs in public bar.

Derwentwater Arms

Low Side. Tel (01433) 630242

Grid ref: 241747

Open: 12-3, 6.30-11; 12-3, 6.30-10.30 Sun.

Beer: Tetley Bitter; plus one guest beer.

Food: From open sandwiches and salads, to a range of traditional hot meals, including a daily specials board. Served lunchtime and evening 'till 9pm in either of two bars (one no-smoking). No food served Sun evening nor Mon (all day).

General: Formerly the Newburgh Arms (which was one of the family titles of the Eyres, who once owned much of the area), this distinctive pub is set on a slightly raised and peculiarly prominent position in the centre of Calver village. It overlooks the cricket pitch, and with wide front windows and terraced seating, it's an excellent place to watch a few overs. The pub has three comfortable bars, two for eating and the third intended more as a games room and dinkers' haunt. The new owners are still making plans for the future, including occasional live music, themed food nights and a new boules pitch. There is disabled access to rear of building.

CASTLETON - Derbyshire

Situated at the dramatic head of the Hope valley, Castleton is popular with walkers, school groups and coach parties, who come here to enjoy the challenging setting. Above ground that means the paths and tracks up to the Lose Hill ridge, culminating in the

1,695 ft summit of Mam Tor; and the dramatic limestone gorge of the Winnats. The hillside immediately to the south reveals the secluded Cave Dale, above which are the remains of Peveril Castle, which can be visited via a steep path. The subterranean attractions are no less impressive, with a series of show caves and caverns, including Treak Cliff and Blue John Caverns. The latter is named after the semi-precious mineral unique to this location. Speedwell Cavern is reached by a boat ride on an underground canal, dug by miners over 200 years ago.

Access: Eight miles north-east of Buxton (A6187).

Bull's Head

Cross Street. Tel (01433) 620256
www.bullsheadcastleton.co.uk
Grid ref: 150829
Open: 11-11; 12-10.30 Sun.

Beer: Robinson's Best Bitter, plus one seasonal Robinson's beer (such as Young Tom).

Food: Set menu (standard choices, but priced reasonably and generous portions) and changing specials chalked up on a board above bar. Served in main bar or separate dining room (half of which is no-smoking), 12-2, 6-9 (Mon-Tues); all day (Wed-Sun, last orders 9pm).

Accommodation: A small campsite (20 tents) is being developed behind the pub, and includes toilet/washing facilities.

General: Recently refurbished, this large, 18th century pub on what is in effect Castleton's main street (near the entrance to the public car park) has an airy, spacious main bar, a games room at the back with pool table, and a tastefully decorated, partitioned dining room. Families welcome; dogs allowed in bar area. Folk sessions on the first Tuesday of each month.

Castle Hotel

Castle Street. Tel (01433) 620578
www.peakland.com/thecastle
Grid ref: 150828
Open: 11-11; 12-10.30 Sun.

Beer: Bass; Tetley Bitter.

Food: The lengthy set menu offers a wide choice of snacks and main meals – the latter including Hunters chicken, baked macaroni cheese and spinach, and beef, mushroom and Bass ale pie. Plenty of vegetarian options. No smoking at the bar and in one large room. Food served 12-10 (Mon-Sat), 12-9 (Sun).

Accommodation: B&B - 9 en-suite double rooms, 3 with 4-poster beds and jacuzzis.

General: This former 17th century coaching inn is associated with a number of ghosts – including a jilted bride called Rose and a former housekeeper called Agnes. Regardless of this it's a popular pub, and so large it has five separate rooms in which to eat and drink. There are tables and chairs out the front, plus a newly laid out terraced garden at the rear, which is heated and lit. Families welcome. Disabled toilet available. Sorry, no dogs. The pub is situated on the corner, opposite the Tourist Information Centre.

George Hotel

Castle Street. Tel (01433) 620238
Grid ref: 150827
Open: 12-3, 6-11 not winter Mon (11-11 summer); 12-3, 6-10.30 (12-10.30 summer) Sun.

Beer: Bass; Wadsworth's 6X; plus one guest beer in summer.

Food: Served 12-2, 7-9 weekdays and all day Sat and Sun 'till 10pm. Food is served in the bar area or in the separate no-smoking dining area. Choices from the specials board may include haggis and stuffed pork fillet with port and redcurrant glaze. Soups and sandwiches are also available at lunchtime for walkers with limited time available.

General: Attractive, 2-roomed pub opposite the Church of St Edmund and near the youth hostel. It began business in 1743 and was originally called the George and Dragon, and still today remains a traditional village inn with oak beams and log fires, families welcome. Dogs allowed in tap room only. Seating outside, front and back.

> *And Noah, he often said to his wife when he sat down to dine. "I don't care where the water goes if it doesn't get into the wine."*
>
> G.K.Chesterton

Olde Cheshire Cheese, Castleton

Olde Cheshire Cheese

How Lane. Tel (01433) 620330
www.peakland.com/cheshirecheese
Grid ref: 152831
Open: 11-11; 12-10.30 Sun.
Beer: Stones Bitter; Worthington Bitter, plus an occasional guest beer.
Food: Full range of hot and cold food, including specials such as locally-caught trout (from Ladybower Reservoir apparently,) giant Yorkshire puddings and various pies (game, brewer's, etc), plus a Sunday roast and vegetarian options. Served 12-9 ('till 9.30pm Fri and Sat), in either the bar or no-smoking restaurant.
Accommodation: B&B - 9 en-suite rooms, 8 double (inc. 2 four-posters) and 1 twin.
General: Pleasant, low-ceilinged pub at eastern (Hope) end of the village, comprising a comfortable front dining room and long L-shaped bar richly and entertainingly decorated with all manner of curios and mementoes, plus a wood-burning stove in the corner. The building dates from 1660, and was opened as a hostelry in 1748 as the Wagon and Horses. Children welcome if eating; no dogs. 'Muddy boots welcome' sign above front door. Live music (usually a folk session) every third Friday of the month.

DIGGLE - Greater Manchester

Located on the very eastern edge of Greater Manchester, this pleasant village nestling below the bulky South Pennines is just outside the National Park boundary, but its proximity to the Pennine Way and newly-reopened Standege canal tunnel

(see Marsden entry for feature) make it worthy of a visit. The pub is actually located at the hamlet of Diglea - turn off the main road through Diggle on to Sam Road and cross the railway.
Access: Three miles north-east of Oldham (off A670).

Diggle Hotel

Digglea Hamlet. Tel (01457) 872741
Grid ref: 007081
Open: 12-3, 5-11; 12-3, 5-10.30 Sun.
Beer: Timothy Taylor's Landlord, Golden Best; Boddingtons Bitter, one guest beer.
Food: Served 12-2.30, 5-9.30 (and all day Sat), there's a full pub menu, and specials such as black pudding bites with apple sauce, steak and ale pudding, and rolled sole with lobster sauce. Also features Sunday lunch and a children's menu.
Accommodation: 3 double rooms.
General: A tall, solid building at the head of the valley, it was a weaver's cottage as long ago as 1789 (the top floor probably contained the looms). It became an ale house and stores when the navvies came to dig the nearby canal and later the railway tunnels. In addition to the main open-plan area there's a small side room for diners, and together with the straightforward home-prepared food and relaxed atmosphere it's a pleasant place. Children welcome if eating; no dogs. Outside seating on front patio.

DUNFORD BRIDGE - South Yorkshire

An isolated, northerly location below Thurlstone Moors in South Yorkshire, four miles south of Holmfirth and five miles west of Penistone (off A628).

Stanhope Arms Inn

Dunford Bridge. Tel (01226) 763104
Grid ref: 157024
Open: 12-3, 7-11; (11-11 Sat winter); 12-10.30 Sun.
Beer: Timothy Taylor's Landlord; Theakston's Best Bitter, and one guest beer (Black Sheep Best Bitter; Caledonian 80/- Ale etc).
Food: Popular and good quality meals and snacks served 12-2, 7-9 (12-6 Sun) throughout pub, and in no-smoking dining room.

From baguettes and light snacks through to range of main meals, including specials such as smoked chicken risotto and bean burritos. Weekday pensioners specials, children's menu, Sunday roast, and à la carte evening selections all feature.

Accommodation: B&B - 5 en-suite rooms.
General: A large and impressive former shooting lodge, with spacious rooms, high ceilings and elegant fireplaces. Apart from the long and rather grand main room, there's a comfortable side area for walkers, a separate dining room, and a cosy snug to the rear of the bar. Families welcome. Outside there's ample seating and a play area for children. Very popular with walkers and cyclists at weekends.

The Trans Pennine Trail

The Stanhope Arms Inn is situated by the Upper Don and Longdendale Trails, which both form sections of the Trans Pennine Trail. This coast to coast route of 213 miles (344km) links Southport (near Liverpool) on the Irish Sea to Hornsea (near Hull) on the North Sea shore. Although there are some urban sections around Hull, Doncaster, Barnsley, Greater Manchester and Merseyside, the TPT utilises existing access corridors such as canal towpaths and country parks, and across much of the central Pennines it follows the trackbed of former railways. As a result the trail can be used by both walkers and cyclists, and some parts are even suitable for horse-riders – a special area at Dunford Bridge is set aside for horses and their boxes. The Trans Pennine Trail also forms the English part of the so-called E8, a trans-European walking route that although still under development is intended to stretch all the way from Galway in the west of Ireland to Istanbul in Turkey. (And you thought the Pennine Way sounded a long way!)

Ale-yard: a trumpet-shaped glass precisely one yard long and containing just over a pint – tradition dictates that the so-called 'yard of ale' has to be drunk in one go without spilling a drop.

EDALE - Derbyshire

Reached via a lane from Hope, Edale comprises a number of different hamlets with a similar name (Upper Booth, Ollerbrook Booth, Barber Booth, Grindsbrook Booth), a 'booth' being an old term for a shepherd's or herdsman's shelter. They're all scattered below the high, stern southern edge of Kinder Scout, the highest point in the Peak District (2,088ft). This is the place to pull on your boots and go exploring, but if you're heading for the high ground make sure you're adequately equipped and drop by the National Park visitor centre to check on the latest weather forecast - it's located between the two pubs near the church.
Access: 2 miles north-west of Castleton (off A6187 at Hope).

Old Nags Head, Edale

Old Nags Head

Edale. Tel (01433) 670291
Grid ref: 123860
Open: 11-11; 12-10.30 Sun.
Beer: Gray's Best Bitter, Premium; Barnsley Bitter.
Food: Hearty helpings of hot and cold food served throughout pub, 12-3, 6-9 (Mon-Fri); 12-9 (Sat); 12-8 (Sun). Specials boards includes homemade rabbit stew, game pie, etc. No smoking in family room. Lounge usually open Saturday evenings.
Accommodation: 2 self-catering cottages.
General: This famous old pub dates back to 1577, and is well-known to generations of walkers as the starting point for the Pennine Way long distance footpath, a rigorous 250-mile route north along the Pennine hills to Scotland. It's still a mecca

North

for booted types - much of the floor remains tiled, and a blackboard advertises 'walkers warmers' (mulled wine, hot toddy, hot lamumba) - but beware crowds at weekends. The sprawling interior includes a family room, tap room and main bar, plus there's a beer garden to the side, and disabled toilet available. Dogs are allowed in the front area only.

Rambler Inn

Edale. (01433) 670268
Grid ref: 123855
Open: 11-11; 12-10.30 Sun.
Beer: Bass; Gray's Premium; Stones Bitter; Theakston's Old Peculier.
Food: Set menu and specials served 12-9 every day, from ciabattas and sandwiches through to steaks, risotto, vegetarian dishes, plus the 'Ramble Combo' (Thai chicken, scampi, duck spring roll, etc). No-smoking area inside.
Accommodation: B&B - 9 en-suite double and twin rooms.
General: Recently refurbished, this large, detached house above the station has plenty of space: outside there are numerous tables and a children's adventure playground, while inside the sleek and colour-coordinated open rooms are more in keeping with a trendy city bar. Families and children welcome; ramp available for disabled access; dogs permitted in certain areas. Every Tuesday the pub plays host to the popular 'Folk Train', when musicians and beer-drinkers enjoy an organised train ride along the Hope Valley and back.

EYAM - Derbyshire

This fascinating, rather strung-out former lead-mining village (pronounced 'Eem') is now famous for just one thing: the Plague. When a local tailor contracted the deadly disease from a damp parcel of cloth from London in 1665 it quickly spread around the village, but rather than escape the community went into a strict, self-imposed quarantine in a selfless attempt to prevent the further spread of the disease. Plague cottages and graves are marked all around the village, and in the parish church of St.Lawrence the Plague Book records the

names of the 350 villagers who perished.
Access: 5 miles north of Bakewell (off A623).

Miners Arms

Water Lane. Tel (01433) 630853
Grid ref: 220765
Open: 11-11; 12-10.30 Sun.
Beer: Stones Bitter; Theakston's Cool Cask, plus one guest beer.
Food: Bar meals served throughout the day, Mon-Sat, and à la carte restaurant (no smoking) open Tues-Sat evenings 7-9, and Sundays 12-6 for traditional roast. Pub also open for morning coffee and afternoon tea in season.
Accommodation: B&B - 7 en-suite rooms (4 doubles, 2 twin, 1 single).
General: A solid, whitewashed inn tucked away off the main square at the eastern end of the village (known as Town End). Although it was built in 1630, before the Plague struck, it is meant to be among the most haunted pubs in the Peak District, and if you sit in the dark, low beamed-ceiling dining room at the back you may find yourself looking twice at a door that blows shut! The two bars at the front are also cosy and comfortable, while there are seats out the front and at the small patio at the rear. No children after 9pm.

FOOLOW - Derbyshire

A small and largely unspoilt limestone village, still retaining three wells that are dressed annually, and a most attractive duck pond. On a popular walking route between Eyam and Great Hucklow.
Access: 5 miles north of Bakewell (off A623)

Bull's Head

Foolow. Tel (01433) 630873
Grid ref: 192768
Open: 12-3, 6.30-11 (closed all day Mon); 12-3, 6-10.30 Sun.
Beer: Black Sheep Best Bitter; Marston's Pedigree; Shepherd Neame Spitfire, and an occasional guest beer.
Food: Full and varied menu served lunchtime and evening until 9pm. Changing specials board, with emphasis on fish and game: roast sea bass, monkfish and prawn stir-fry, game casserole, honeyed guinea fowl with plum sauce. Eat in bars or separate no

smoking dining area (formerly the stable).
Accommodation: 3 en-suite rooms (2 doubles, 1 twin).

General: A large, traditional country pub, the Bull's Head stands at the centre of this quiet village, and despite its pink-washed exterior inside it's largely unspoilt, with stone-flagged floors and an oak-panelled dining room. Families with children, muddy boots and dogs all welcome, plus there's a wheelchair entrance at the back and a disabled toilet available. Outside the front there's a few tables; and every Friday evening and Sunday lunchtime a pianist tinkles away (usually with vocal accompaniment on Fridays).

> *Remember that Peak District pubs can get very busy during peak times (summer weekends and bank holidays especially) so if you're eating consider booking a table in advance (not possible at every pub).*

FROGGATT EDGE - Derbyshire

North of Calver the densely-wooded slopes of the Derwent valley culminate in a long, flat escarpment known as Froggatt Edge. An easy and panoramic track runs its entire length, or for a different perspective you can follow the riverside footpath far below between Froggatt and Calver.

Chequers Inn

Froggatt Edge (on A625 - formerly B6054).
Tel (01433) 630231
Grid ref: 247761
Open: 11-3, 6-11; 11-11 Sat; 12-10.30 Sun.
Beer: Marston's Pedigree; Theakston's Best Bitter.
Food: Popular, high-quality dining pub, with specials that include dishes such as whole grilled skate wing with capers and lemon & chive butter, and roast duck breast with oriental savoy cabbage and hoisin dressing. Food served 12-2, 6-9.30 (Mon-Fri), and all day at weekends. No-smoking dining room at one end. Booking advisable at weekends.
Accommodation: B&B - 6 en-suite rooms (4 double, 2 twin).
General: This former coaching pub dates from 1735, but an even earlier version is believed to have provided refreshment

on the long and what was no doubt very tiring packhorse route out of the valley (a horse mounting block is still evident outside the pub). Inside, the main bar has a wooden floor and solid fuel stove, while at the other end of the refurbished building the no-smoking dining room houses 'The Chequers Paintings' - changing displays and exhibitions by mostly local artists. Patio seating and terraced garden set into the hillside to the rear. Children in no-smoking dining room only; no dogs.

GLOSSOP - Derbyshire

A large and busy gritstone town sitting at the western end of the Snake Pass, and a popular place of departure for weekend walkers heading for the wild heights of Bleaklow and Kinder Scout. In terms of history Old Glossop, to the north-east of the present centre, has a parish church, a medieval market cross and some fine old houses. However, most of Glossop's shops and two dozen pubs and clubs are found in the more modern part dating from 1830, planned by the Duke of Norfolk as a new town for local textile workers. There's more on Glossop's industrial past at the Heritage Centre (on Henry Street), and general details from the Tourist Information Centre on Victoria Street (tel 01457 855920). The latter used to be the entrance to the massive Howardtown Mills, which in its heyday stretched for $1/4$ mile.

Bull's Head

102 Church Street, Old Glossop.
Tel (01457) 853291
Grid ref: 042949
Open: 11-11; 12-10.30 Sun.
Beer: Robinson's Best Bitter, Old Stockport Bitter.
Food: Half the pub is taken up with a popular Indian restaurant and take-away, where high-quality meals served in generous portions can be chosen from a huge menu (over 100 dishes) taking in balti, karahi, rogan josh, samber, madras, schazlik, and so on. There are three separate dining rooms (two no-smoking), open 5.30-10.30 Mon-Sat, and 4.30-10 (Sun).
General: Dating from around 1780, much

North

of this traditional old pub remains unchanged. There are two small, front rooms, with an open fire, board games and upright piano, then beyond the bar at the far end the Indian restaurant begins. Legend has it that a tunnel once linked the pub with the church opposite, allowing the monks to flee in time of difficulty, although what they would make of the sight and smell of a plate of steaming chicken madras if they surfaced today is anyone's guess. Families welcome; dogs in tap room only.

Friendship Inn

3 Arundel Street. Tel (01457) 855277
Grid ref: 033943
Open: 4 (11 Sat)-11; 12-3, 7-10.30 Sun.
Beer: Robinson's Best Bitter, Mild.
General: Charming corner pub off High Street West/A57, five minutes walk from town centre. Comfortable oak-panelled main room, decorated with various cricket memorabilia (including some fine prints and paintings). Beyond the gleaming semi-circular bar, is a pool room; then outside is an attractive, enclosed garden area, with terraces, pot plants and a small bar that sees occasional summertime use. Children welcome 'till 8.30pm; dogs allowed inside.

Nag's Head

19 Charlestown Road. Tel (01457) 853163
Grid ref: 034935
Open: 11-11; 12-10.30 Sun.
Beer: No hand-pull beer at present.
Food: Served 12-3, 5-10 (weekends all day until 10pm). Eat in bar area, including no-smoking section, or restaurant (also no-smoking) which is licensed until midnight. Specials include chicken salsa and mozarella and leek macaroni. Popular carvery from Fri-Sun; children's menu is available.
General: Family-friendly pub five minutes walk south of town centre on main road towards Hayfield. One large, open-plan lounge bar, with corner stage (regular live music). Separate conservatory restaurant, and traditional tap room with pool table. Children welcome until 8pm, or later if dining. Disabled toilet facilities. Groups are welcome. Dogs in tap room only.

Prince of Wales

Mill Street, Milltown. Tel (01457) 864679
Grid ref: 038941
Open: 4.30 (11 Sat)-11; 12-10.30 Sun.
Beer: Marston's Bitter, Pedigree, plus one guest beer (from breweries such as Morrells, Wychwood, Phoenix, etc).
Food: Full range of hot and cold pub food, served weekday evenings 'till 8pm, and Sunday 12-6. The lower room is being converted into a no-smoking dining area.
General: Pleasant public house on side turning east of Glossop centre (off High Street East/A57). The main bar has open seating, dark ceiling beams and brass decorations. To the front is a separate pool room, and at the rear is the new dining room (beer garden out the back). Range of malt whiskies. Children are admitted 'till 7.30pm; dogs permitted inside.

Star Inn Ale House

2 Howard Street. Tel (01457) 853072
Grid ref: 036943
Open: 11-11; 12-10.30 Sun.
Beer: Boddington's Bitter; Timothy Taylor's Landlord; Pictish Gold, plus three guest beers from breweries such as Manchester's Phoenix Brewery, Kelham Island from Sheffield.
General: This late 19th century corner building near the station is today a comfortable but unfussy place for the real ale connoisseur. There's long wall seats and bare wooden floors, plus a cosy tap room at the end, and despite occasional free soup or snacks on a weekend afternoon the absence of pub food and numbered tables is quite welcome. Dogs allowed inside.

GREAT HUCKLOW - Derbyshire

This peaceful village nestles at the foot of Hucklow Edge, over the back of which is a gliding field that is the base for the Derbyshire and Lancashire Gliding Club. It was founded in 1935 and is one of the oldest in England, and as you gaze upwards the sight of the huge but silent craft circling the thermals is quite arresting.
Access: Six miles north-west of Bakewell (off A623).

Queen Anne

Great Hucklow. Tel (01298) 871246
Grid ref: 177779
Open: 12-2.30 (3 Sat), 6-11;
12-2.30/3, 7-10.30 Sun.
Beer: Mansfield Bitter; Barnsley Bitter, plus one guest beer.
Food: Bar meals served every lunchtime and evening until 9pm (one bar no smoking). Menu ranges from sandwiches and jacket potatoes to home-made pies and soups, and rice dishes such as tropical vegetable curry, lamb balti, and Moroccan lamb with apricot.
Accommodation: B&B - 2 en-suite rooms (1 double, 1 twin) in self-contained building next-door.
General: Friendly, unspoilt village local, consisting of one main bar with large open fireplace and cosy fireside benches, leading out to a secluded beer garden at the rear with pleasant views across the fields. At the front is a separate, tiny bar. The pub dates back to 1621, and just as it once hosted passing packhorse teams and other travellers it now receives walkers and other visitors (families welcome, dogs allowed inside).

> *"You can't be a REAL Country unless you have a BEER or an airline. It helps if you have some kind of football team, or some nuclear weapons, but at the very least you need a BEER."*
>
> Frank Zappa

GRINDLEFORD - Derbyshire

Located mainly on the west bank of the River Derwent, Grindleford enjoys good views of the wooded valley towards the Longshaw estate, and the rocky shelf of Froggatt Edge. Just north of the three-arched bridge a riverside path leads to Upper Padley, which sits at the foot of the delightful oak woodland of Padley Gorge. Here you'll also find Padley Chapel, where during a tide of anti-Catholic sentiment in the 1580s two Roman Catholic priests were arrested and taken to Derby where they were hanged, drawn and quartered. An annual pilgrimage takes place here each summer in their memory.

Access: 2 1/2 miles south of Hathersage (on B6521).

Maynard Arms Hotel

Main Road. Tel (01433) 630321
Grid ref: 248784
Open: 11-3, 5.30-11; 12-10.30 Sun.
Beer: Marston's Pedigree; Morland Old Speckled Hen; Boddingtons Bitter; Timothy Taylor's Landlord.
Food: Decent pub food choices in the Longshaw Bar, 12-2, 6-9.30 (Mon-Sat), 12-9.30 (Sun), or more exclusive menu in the Padley Restaurant (12-2, 7-9.30, bookings advisable at weekends). Bar menu includes rack of pork, mackerel and trout, lamb shoulder, etc; and ever-changing if pricey restaurant menu includes likes of wild salmon, calves livers, etc. No smoking in restaurant and part of bar.
Accommodation: B&B - 10 en-suite rooms (8 doubles, 2 twin).
General: Imposing Victorian hotel situated on the B6521 1/2 mile north of Grindleford bridge. Named after a family whose distant descendants include Sir Richard Maynarde, who fought for King Henry V at Agincourt, the hotel was built in 1901 when the Sheffield-Manchester railway finally emerged from the new 6,230-yard Totley tunnel. Externally, the building looks rather stern and haughty, but inside it's all plush carpets, oak panels and leather seats, and over the years its hosted banquets and balls, and guests have included the Duke of Devonshire and Sir Paul McCartney.

Sir William Hotel

Sir William Road. Tel (01433) 630303
www.sirwilliamhotel.com
Grid ref: 244777
Open: 11-11; 12-10.30 Sun.
Beer: Tetley Bitter, plus up to three guest beers such as Timothy Taylor's Landlord; Marston's Pedigree, etc.
Food: Extensive, quality menu, served in main bar or no-smoking restaurant from 12-2, 6.30-9.30 (Mon-Sat), 12-9 (Sun). Choice of light snacks including range of ciabattas and baguettes, through to varied main courses (specials include baked trout, rabbit stew, tobasco roast poussin, seared

North

scallops); plus good wine list.

Accommodation: B&B - 7 en-suite rooms (3 doubles, 3 twin, 1 family).

General: A large, imposing pub looking down on the village from the Hathersage road (B6001), next to the school. Originally called the Bluebell Inn, it acquired its present name in 1925, probably after Sir William Savile, Lord of the Manor of Eyam in the 1600s. However, it may also refer to Sir William Chambers Bagshawe, a 17th century local landowner who purportedly rebuilt the road across the nearby hill (which still bears his name) in order to link his two estates. The pub is high-ceilinged and airy, with pleasant views over the Derwent valley, especially from the garden terrace, plus there's a small tap room with an upright piano. Families welcome; live music (60s/70s) every Sunday evening; dogs in tap room only.

HATHERSAGE - Derbyshire

In the churchyard of St Michael and All Angels, just off and above the main street, is an oversized grave said to be that of Little John, 'friend and lieutenant of Robin Hood', as the modern gravestone puts it. It's worth a look, even if you are a diehard sceptic. The skyline is dominated by the brooding crags of Stanage Edge, a long-time mecca for climbers, and with outdoor shops prominent in the town's main street you'll see many booted and cagouled walkers setting off for a day on the moors or dales. Charlotte Bronte stayed at Hathersage Vicarage in 1845, and is believed to have used North Lees Hall as the model for Thornfield Hall in 'Jane Eyre'.

Access: On A6187, 6 miles north of Baslow.

Little John Hotel

Station Road. Tel (01433) 630225
Grid ref: 230814,
Open: 11-11; 12-10.30 Sun.

Beer: Four changing cask beers (such as Everards Tiger; Elgoods Cambridge Bitter; Courage Directors, etc).

Food: Full range of hot and cold meals (from hot baguettes to mixed grills) in portions generous enough to satisfy even the hungriest rambler. Served from 12-2, 6-10

weekdays and all day weekends 'till 10pm on Saturday and 9pm on Sunday (8pm in winter).

Accommodation: 6 rooms (5 doubles and 1 twin, 3 of them en-suite), plus 4 new self-catering cottage units behind the pub.

General: Formerly the Station Hotel, this old-fashioned pub with high ceilings, deep leather chairs and stained glass windows consists of a tap room (with a pool and bar billiards table), and a lounge and snug, part of which is no-smoking. Children very welcome in the latter; ramp and disabled toilet available. Dogs allowed inside.

Millstone Inn, 1939

Millstone Inn

Sheffield Road (A6187). Tel (01433) 650258
Grid ref: 242807
Open: 11.30-3, 6-11; 11-11 Sat; 12-10.30 Sun.

Beer: Black Sheep Best Bitter; Timothy Taylor Landlord, plus one guest beer.

Food: Standard range of pub food, weekend carvery, etc, served lunchtime and evenings ('till 9.30pm), all day at weekends, in bar or no-smoking dining area.

Accommodation: B&B – 6 en-suite rooms (4 doubles, 2 family rooms), and a self-catering flat that sleeps up to 6.

General: Situated a mile south-east of Hathersage and high on the hillside, the pub takes its name from the distinctive millstones that were quarried from above the Derwent valley, and which are now incorporated as the Peak National Park's logo. Originally a 17th century farmhouse, the pub was rebuilt in 1929 in what can only be described as an incongruous, 3-storey mix of mock Tudor, Georgian and Regency styles. Walkers and families welcome; small (fenced) outside seating area by roadside, and opposite by car park on hillside. Live bands play in the function room every last Friday of the month.

Plough Inn

Leadmill Bridge, Hathersage. Tel (01433) 650319
Grid ref: 234804
Open: 11-11; 12-10.30 Sun.

Beer: Theakston's Best Bitter, and three guest beers (such as Adnams Bitter and Black Sheep Best Bitter).

Food: A popular eating pub, there's a choice of traditional hot and cold pub food in the split-level bar, or a more wide-ranging menu in the no-smoking restaurant. The latter includes dishes such as goats cheese and sweet potato ravioli. Served 11.30-2.30 and 6.30-9.30 (9 on Sunday).

Accommodation: B&B - 5 en-suite doubles/twins.

General: This smart, 17th century inn is situated close to the bridge over the River Derwent, half a mile south of Hathersage on the B6001. Originally the waterside site housed a mill (first a corn mill, then for lead smelting), but later it became a farmstead. There are a few seats by the road out the front, and to the side is a pleasant hedged, sunken garden. Children allowed inside if eating. No dogs.

There are approx. 1.600 miles of public rights of way in the Peak District National Park

Scotsman's Pack

School Lane. Tel (01433) 630253.
www.peakland.com/scotsmanspack
Grid ref: 235817
Open: 11.30-3, 6-11; 11-11 Sat; 12-10.30 Sun.

Beer: Burtonwood Bitter, Top Hat, plus one guest beer.

Food: A popular place to eat, the blackboard choices are served throughout the long bar, which includes a no-smoking section, between 12-2 and 6-9 Mon-Fri, and 12-9 at weekends. Among the specials are bacon steak with Cumberland sauce, grilled salmon with egg noodles and sweet chilli sauce. Booking advisable for weekends.

Accommodation: B&B - 5 en-suite rooms (3 doubles, 1 twin, 1 single)

General: Named after the packmen or 'travelling drapers' who used to come down from Scotland with their tweeds and woollens and walk from village to village selling their wares. Although an inn existed on this site for many centuries, serving the packmen and other travellers on the old road to Sheffield, the present building dates from 1900 and is a comfortable, open-plan affair designed as much for diners as for drinkers. There's a small seating area by the stream to the side of the building. Live jazz every first Monday evening of the month.

HAYFIELD - Derbyshire

Hayfield nestles under the dark, bulky height of Kinder Scout and is a popular base for walkers looking to explore the more wilder and remote Dark Peak. The village once echoed to the sound of wool weaving and calico printing, and until the 1970s bypass was built, the incessant traffic was a problem. But today it's a quiet and happy mix of pubs, cafes and local shops; and a small building behind the George provides the base for the local mountain rescue team. For more details on Hayfield see www.hayfield.uk.net

Access: 4 miles north of Chapel-en-le-Frith (on A624).

George Hotel

Church Street. Tel (01663) 743691
www.thegeorgehayfield.com
Grid ref: 037868
Open: 12-3, 5.30-11; 11-11 Sat; 12-10.30 Sun.

Beer: Burtonwood Bitter, and occasional Burtonwood seasonal beers.

Food: Well-priced pub grub (fish, jacket potatoes, pies, torpedo sandwiches) served lunchtimes only 12-2 (3 at weekends) including Hiker's Hotpot of a bread roll and pickled red cabbage. Decent coffee available via authentic espresso machine.

Accommodation: B&B - 6 double rooms.

General: Cosy, dark intimate pub dating from the 16th century, and until 1830 was called the Mail Inn, as letters were dispatched from here every Saturday morning. The large, stone-flagged main room features a beautiful Lancashire range, and the three smaller bars include a pool room at the rear. Live music most weekends, including jazz on Sunday afternoons. Small garden at rear; no children after 8pm. Dogs are allowed inside.

The Kinder Scout Mass Trespass

Today the sight of groups of walkers puffing their way up the steep paths and tracks to the wild moorland tops is commonplace, and of course the pubs and shops and B&Bs of places like Hayfield rely heavily on their trade. But access that we now take for granted was not always so, and it was won at a price. On 24th April 1932 the heather slopes above Hayfield were the scene of the famous Kinder Scout Mass Trespass, when a group of young ramblers from Manchester demonstrated against a lack of access to the private grouse moors. As they returned from their successful and peaceful protest they were stopped by the police who made several arrests. Six were later charged with 'riotous assembly' and subsequently jailed, but the campaign to open up the hills was set in motion. A plaque commemorating their efforts can be found in Bowden Bridge quarry (now used as a car park by ramblers) on Kinder Road beyond the Sportsman pub.

Royal Hotel

Market Street. Tel (01663) 742721
Grid ref: 037869
Open: 12-3, 6-11; 11-11 Sat; 12-10.30 Sun.
Beer: Tetley Bitter; Morland Old Speckled Hen; Marston's Pedigree, plus up to five guest beers.
Food: Wide-ranging set menu of hot and cold meals and snacks, plus changing daily specials board (look out for the fish dishes). Food served throughout large public bar area (partly no-smoking), or no-smoking restaurant at rear.
Accommodation: B&B - 12 en-suite rooms.
General: Large, handsome building beside the village cricket pitch. In front the River Sett now flows down a reinforced channel, since previous floods have demolished bridges and in 1748 it even swept away bodies buried in the local graveyard. The hotel, which was previously the vicarage, dates from 1755, and as you step inside you're struck by the spaciousness of the comfortable oak-panelled bars. Children allowed inside until 9pm (separate family area). No dogs. Patio seating out the front by car park.

Sportsman

Kinder Road. Tel (01663) 741565
Grid ref: 045867
Open: 12-3, 7-11 (closed Mon); 12-3, 7-10.30 Sun.
Beer: Thwaites Best Bitter, and a regular Thwaites seasonal beer.
Food: Quality hot and cold food from set menu (including filled French bread and club sandwiches) plus changing specials board – such as Somerset pork chops with onions and apples casseroled, and Oxford John (lamb fillet panfried in port with redcurrants). Served 12-2 and 7-9 (except Mon) throughout bars. No-smoking areas on request.
Accommodation: B&B - 6 en-suite rooms (4 double, 2 twin).
General: Situated on a small no-through road east of the village towards Kinder Reservoir (leave the centre of Hayfield on Bank Street and follow the sign for the Camping and Caravanning Club site), this smart and attractive inn is justly popular for its food, served to a backdrop of open fires and piped jazz. Everyone welcome (from families and dogs to walkers), plus there's a small area of garden to the side.

For the latest news and information on the Peak National Park check out www.peakdistrict.org

HOLME - West Yorkshire

A high and attractive hamlet on the extreme north-eastern edge of the Peak National Park. It's surrounded by bracing walking country, including the boggy morass of Black Hill, or for a slightly gentler option try the Holme Valley Circular Walk and Kirklees Way which both go through Holme.
Access: Two miles south-west of Holmfirth on A6024.

Fleece Inn

Holme. Tel (01484) 683449
Grid ref: 107058
Open: 12-3, 6-11; 11-11 Sat; 12-10.30 Sun.
Beer: Burtonwood Bitter, Top Hat, plus one guest beer such as Charles Wells Bombardier; Wychwood's Hobgoblin, etc.
Food: Varied range of mouth-watering meals and snacks (including sandwiches

and baguettes), from either lunchtime evening or Sunday lunch menus. Evening specials include cannelloni ricotta and aubergine parmesan, while the immensely popular 'food theme nights' have ranged from Mexican to Thai and Indian. Children's portions available. Served 12-2 (3 at weekends), 6-9 (9.30 Fri and Sat), not Sun eve. No-smoking areas.

General: Attractive and surprisingly spacious old village pub, very welcoming and comfortable. Open-plan main area allows space for diners, but side area by wood-burning stove is as much for conversation and drinking. Carefully furnished, including displays of pottery and crafts. Popular with walkers and cyclists. Families welcome; ramp for front door and plans for disabled toilet; no dogs inside. Roadside benches at front.

HOPE - Derbyshire

The Hope Valley extends westwards towards the unmistakable bulk of Mam Tor, but before Castleton you pass through the small settlement of Hope itself. The parish church was mentioned in the Domesday Book, and before that the Angles and Saxons worshipped on the same site. It was once the custom that on the declaration of the banns prior to a marriage the clerk would call out: "God speed the couple well!" Like nearby Castleton, there are a number of inviting paths that lead up to the hills and ridges that surround the valley, most notably to the immediate north towards Win Hill and its equally distinctive neighbour Lose Hill.

Access: 3 1/2 miles west of Hathersage (on A6187).

Cheshire Cheese Inn

Edale Road. Tel (01433) 620381
Grid ref: 171841
Open: 12-3, 6.30-11; 11-11 Sat;
12-4, 6.30-10.30 Sun.

Beer: Black Sheep Best Bitter; Barnsley Bitter; Timothy Taylor's Landlord; Whim Hartington Bitter, plus one guest beer (often from the Wentworth brewery).

Food: Snacks and meals served 12-2 (2.30 weekends), 6.30-9, in two small bars

or no-smoking dining area. Daily specials board includes likes of pies, stir fry, vegetarian options (courgette crumble, tuna bake, etc), and 'the Cheshire Cheese mammoth mixed grill' suitable for even the hungriest walker.

Accommodation: B&B - 1 en-suite double.

General: A charming 16th century pub situated 1/2 mile out of Hope on the Edale Road. Apparently it takes its name from the former salt-carrying packhorse trains who used to pay for their overnight lodgings in cheese, and indeed old cheese hooks are still on display. It's a cosy, unpretentious pub, with real fires, decent beers, a garden at the rear, and is deservedly popular with passing walkers. Children allowed in eating area only; dogs allowed in bar.

It's in the can

Until 1834 there was a high duty on glass and people used to keep their own bottles to re-fill as needed. When the duty was removed it was economical for brewers to bottle beer in quantity. The bottles had simple black and white labels to identify the beer and brewer. As colour printing developed and became cheaper, the labels became more attractive and brand images were developed (the Bass red triangle being the oldest trade mark). In the 1870s it became possible to print directly onto tinplate, and many items were sold in canned form. The problem with beer is that it needs to be canned under pressure, this caused the seams of early cans to split. Beer is also corrosive and would react with the inner tinplate coating of the steel can. After experimenting with various coatings, and with a stronger can construction, the problems were eventually solved. The first canned beer was available in America in 1935. Two types of cans were available, the flat topped as we know today, and a cone-top (like the old Brasso tins). The cone-tops were able to be filled using existing bottling lines, thus saving money for the brewer. However their use ceased in the 1950s. Modern two piece beer cans are extruded from a slug of aluminium or steel, and are printed after production.

North

Woodroffe Arms Hotel

1 Castleton Road. Tel (01433) 620351
www.woodroffearms.co.uk
Grid ref: 172835
Open: 11-11; 12-10.30 Sun.

Beer: Stones Bitter; John Smith's Bitter; Marston's Pedigree.

Food: Wide range of decent, if standard pub food, with separate lunch and evening specials board. Served 12-2, 6.30-9.30 (Mon- Sat), 12-3. 6-9.30 (Sun), including lunchtime/afternoon carvery.

Accommodation: B&B - 3 en-suite rooms (2 doubles, 1 twin).

General: Named after an influential local family who can be traced back to the 15th century, and who once held the title of King's Foresters of the Peak. This tall, solid pub next to the parish church of St Peter has a wide front bar (open fire) that leads through to a conservatory restaurant (no-smoking), with outside seating and children's swings. Dogs allowed inside A courtesy bus operates for customers staying in local B&Bs and campsites.

> *"It's my opinion, sir, that this meeting is drunk!"* Mr Stiggins, in Pickwick Papers by Charles Dickens

LADYBOWER RESERVOIR - Derbyshire

Ladybower Inn

Ladybower Reservoir (on A57, two miles north of Bamford). Tel (01433) 651241
Grid ref: 204865
Open: 11-11; 12-10.30 Sun.

Beer: Barnsley Bitter, plus one guest beer in summer.

Food: Large menu of hot and cold food served 12-2.30, 5-9.30 (Mon-Thurs), all day till 9.30 (Fri-Sun), including Sunday roasts, vegetarian dishes and children's choices. Main meals include braised steak in Guinness and orange, and pheasant supremes in a red wine sauce on mash. No-smoking dining area.

General: Roadside inn at the far eastern end of Ladybower Reservoir. Originally further up Ladybower Brook, the inn was re-sited over a century ago. It consists of one, long open-plan room, with a separate dining area at one end. The walls are decorated with various angling memorabilia and photos of Lancaster bombers flying over the Upper Derwent dams, since the reservoirs were used for pilot training before the 'Dambuster' raids. Walkers, cyclists and fell-runners all use the pub, and children are welcome up to 9pm. No dogs inside.

The Upper Derwent Reservoirs

To satisfy the growing thirst of Sheffield and the cities of the East Midlands three large reservoirs were built in the Upper Derwent valley in the first half of the 20th century: Howden (completed in 1912), Derwent (1916) and Ladybower (1943). The construction of the great dams was a huge undertaking, and many of the navvies were housed in the so-called 'Tin Town' at Birchinlee, a self-contained community of huts and temporary buildings that lasted for over 15 years. Sadly the flooding of the valleys meant that several farmsteads and the old villages of Derwent and Ashopton had to be abandoned, and fine buildings like Ashopton Inn and the 17th century Derwent Hall were demolished. But in the unusually dry summer of 1959 the water levels dropped sufficiently for a local man to recover stones from the family farm that he had been forced to give up 16 years before. He ended up using them as a rockery outside his new home in Ashbourne! When full Ladybower Reservoir holds 6,310 million gallons, and covers 600 acres.

> *"In water one sees one's own face, but in wine one beholds the heart of another."* French Proverb

LANGSETT - South Yorkshire

Langsett doesn't actually consist of much more than a pub, self-catering youth hostel and a few other buildings, but for all that it's well worth a visit to enjoy a stroll through the reservoir-side pines, or perhaps a longer and more adventurous walk on to the moors.

Access: four miles west of Penistone on A616.

Waggon and Horses

Langsett. Tel (01226) 763147
www.langsettinn.com
Grid ref: 213004
Open: 12-3, 6.30-11; 12-3, 6.30-10.30 Sun.
Beer: Courage Directors; Theakston's Best Bitter.
Food: Traditional range of snacks and meals, with home-made pies something of a speciality: chicken and asparagus, meat and potato, followed by their renown bilberry pie. Served 12-2, 6.30-9 (no food Sun or Mon evenings) in bar or handsome no-smoking dining room. Can get very busy at weekends.
Accommodation: B&B - 1 double, 2 twin (all en-suite).
General: Welcoming and cosy one-room old pub by main road. Built in 1809, it's been a popular stopover with travellers, whether enjoying the open fire in winter or views over Langsett Reservoir from the garden at the rear. Every year on the Oct/Nov full moon the 'Hunters Moon' is celebrated with live music, dancing and fireworks.

LITTLE HAYFIELD - Derbyshire

An attractive hamlet one mile north of Hayfield on A624. The pub here is named after Lantern Pike, a National Trust owned hill nearby. There is a concessionary path to the summit, where there are panoramic views towards the Sett valley and Kinder.

Lantern Pike Inn

Glossop Road (A624),
Little Hayfield. Tel (01663) 747590
Grid ref: 034883
Open: 12-3, 6-11; 11-11 Sat; 12-10.30 Sun.
Beer: Timothy Taylor's Landlord; Boddington's Bitter; Flowers IPA, plus occasional guest beers.
Food: Reasonably-priced set menu, including children's and pensioner's choices, plus daily specials including lemon sole stuffed with crab meat, oriental pork with cashew nuts, and chicken & coriander with sweet potato. Served in bars or in the no-smoking dining area.
Accommodation: B&B - 5 en-suite rooms (3 double, 2 twin).

General: Friendly, cosy pub off main road north of Hayfield. The 18th century building on the former Buxton-Old Glossop turnpike is stuffed full of curiosities, including a decorated glass panel illuminated from behind, plus a signed letter from Coronation Street's original scriptwriter and former local Tony Warren. He supposedly based some of the show's first characters on the pub's regulars. Popular with walkers (no dogs inside), there's a beer garden to the rear, and children welcome 'till 9pm.

LITTLE HUCKLOW - Derbyshire

A peaceful hamlet located off the Bradwell-Tideswell road (B6049), three miles from Castleton.

Olde Bull's Head

Little Hucklow. Tel (01298) 871097
www.yeoldebullshead.co.uk
Grid ref: 165786
Open: 12-3, 6-11; 12-3, 6-10.30 Sun.
Beer: Tetley Bitter; John Smith's Magnet.
Food: Served in bars between 12-3 and 7-9pm every day, the food is prepared to order (and in generous proportions), ranging from sandwiches and baguettes to stilton and vegetable bake, Barnsley chop and what they modestly call 'the Bull's Head famous gammon steak'.
Accommodation: B&B - 2 en-suite double rooms across the lane converted from former outhouses.
General: Attractive and historic whitewashed building, reputedly dating back to the 12th century and claiming to be the 5th oldest pub in England. There are two small dark bars, with open fires, oak beams and great thick walls, and upstairs is another small room known as the Cave. Previous innkeepers were also miners, and there was once a shaft in the pub's cellar that connected it with the mine below! Families welcome; scattering of outside picnic tables with pleasant views across the fields and up to the gliders circling on the thermals high above.

> *"There are two things that will be believed of any man whatsoever, and one of them is that he has taken to drink."* Booth Tarkinton

Longshaw – Marsden

North

LONGSHAW - Derbyshire

The National Trust's Longshaw Estate covers 1,600 acres high on the eastern rim of the Derwent valley between Grindleford and Hathersage. Below the former shooting lodge is Longshaw Meadow, the venue each September for historic sheepdog trials. They began in 1898, apparently to settle an argument between farmers and shepherds in the Fox House over who owned the best sheepdog. Nearby a popular footpath runs along the lovely Burbage Brook, which suddenly tumbles from the open moorland through the wooded slopes of Padley Gorge. The Fox House is situated by the junction of the A6187/B6521 near the Estate visitor centre, while the Grouse Inn is a mile to the south on the A625.

Fox House

Hathersage Road (A6187 – formerly A625).
Tel (01433) 630374
Grid ref: 266803
Open:11-11, 12-10.30 Sun.
Beer: Bass; Stones Bitter.
Food: Wide-ranging set menu (with option of 'smaller plates' and 'larger plates'). plus specials board. Main dishes include likes of seafood salad, lemon chicken, filo pastry basket with roasted butternut squash, spinach and pine nuts. Served 12-10 daily (9.30 Sun). Like most Vintage Inns pubs the majority of the building is no-smoking.
Accommodation: B&B -10 en-suite rooms (7 doubles, 2 family, 1 single).
General: Built in the 1770s as a two-roomed cottage, this moorland inn also served as a home for local shepherds; and in particularly bad weather the sheep would even be accommodated, when straw was laid over the tap room floor for the night! However, times have changed somewhat, and now this very popular moorland inn is run by a national pub chain and the building has been modernised throughout. There are a series of small rooms and alcoves, incorporating a wheelchair lift to upper dining area, as well as disabled toilets. Families and walkers welcome, but no dogs inside. Some outside seating by car park.

Grouse Inn

Longshaw (on A625 formerly B6054, roughly 3 miles north-east of Calver).
Tel (01433) 630423
Grid ref: 257779
Open: 12-3, 6-11; 11-11 Sat; 12-10.30 Sun.
Beer: Marston's Pedigree; Banks's Bitter, plus one guest beer.
Food: Hot and cold food served every lunchtime, Wed-Sun evening (until 9pm). Usual range of sandwiches and bar food, plus specials such as spinach and walnut pancake, brie and broccoli pithivier, and tumeric chicken.
General: Sitting isolated amid the high moorland at the northern end of Froggatt Edge, this is a good place from which to admire the splendid views across the upper Derwent valley – although in the depths of winter you'll appreciate the cosiness of the wood-burning stove instead. Outside it's a tough-looking, rather austere building, but inside, the main bar is comfortable and pleasantly-furnished, and there's a back bar (for walkers, etc), plus a patio area where barbecues, music and occasional theme nights take place. Children in the back bar only; wheelchair ramp from car park; a few outside seats.

MARSDEN - West Yorkshire

A small Yorkshire milltown located on the northernmost fringe of the Dark Peak. To the south and west is a high ring of bleak, open Pennine moorland, while to the north-east the Colne valley stretches out towards Huddersfield seven miles away. Look out for the annual Marsden Jazz Festival, which usually takes place each autumn, and the newly-opened Standedge visitor centre (see canal feature below).

Great Western

Manchester Road. Tel (01484) 844315
Grid ref: 025099
Open: 12-3, 6.30-11; (closed Mon); 11-11 Sat; 12-10.30 Sun.
Beer: Tetleys Bitter; Worthington Bitter; Cains Bitter; Black Sheep Best Bitter.
Food: Full set menu and specials board, including suet pudding (lamb and mint, chicken and leek), and home-made fish

pie (cod, salmon and smoked mackerel in a rich cheese sauce topped with new potatoes). Served when open, last orders around 9-9.30, in bar area or large dining room (open Fri-Sun).

General: A remote and windswept pub by the busy A62, sitting on top of the moors high above Marsden. A little to the west is the Pennine Way, while opposite is Redbrook Reservoir where a few hardy souls occasionally sail. Their antics can be viewed from the warmth and safety of the pub's two pleasant, if unremarkable front rooms. Families welcome; no dogs.

A canal tunnel with a difference

When, in the 1790s, engineers working on the new Huddersfield Narrow Canal came up against the Pennines there was only one option: go straight underneath it. As a result, Thomas Telford's 3 $1/2$ mile Standedge Tunnel was hewn out of solid rock and became the longest, deepest and also the highest canal tunnel in Britain. After falling into disuse last century this remarkable thoroughfare has been fully restored, and a former transhipment warehouse by the eastern entrance near Marsden transformed into a new visitor centre. There are now boat trips into the tunnel, which emerges at Diggle in Greater Manchester, plus a range of interactive displays and exhibitions. For more details contact Standedge Visitor Centre, Waters Road, Marsden, tel 01484 844298; www.standedge.co.uk

---

Riverhead Brewery Tap

2 Peel Street. Tel (01484) 841270
Grid ref: 048117
Open: 5 (4 Fri)-11; 11-11 Sat; 12-10.30 Sun.

Beer: This unusual and interesting pub brews its own beers on the premises (you can view the full mash brewery through an observation window at the back), and each beer is named after local reservoirs, the higher their altitude the higher the respective gravity of the beer: Sparth Mild, Butterley Bitter, Deer Hill Porter, Cupwith Light Bitter, Black Moss Stout, March Haigh Special Bitter, Redbrook Premium Bitter. Seasonal beers are occasionally prepared

for events such as the annual Cuckoo Day and Jazz festivals. Also look out for Ruby Tuesday (strong pink cider made in Yorkshire), and an unusual selection of malt whiskies.

General: Sympathetically renovated former former Co-op stores, with scrubbed floorboards and tasteful lighting. Spacious and high-ceilinged, with a disabled toilet at the rear. There's no pub food, jukeboxes or slot machines, but rather it's very much a haven for good conversation and an appreciation of quality beer. When it gets busy a quieter overspill room upstairs is available, which is also used as a meeting room for local groups. Dogs allowed inside.

Swan

7 Station Road. Tel (01484) 844308
Grid ref: 047118
Open: 12-4.30, 7-11; 11-11 Sat; 12-10.30 Sun.

Beer: Thwaites Bitter, Mild, plus one seasonal Thwaites beer.

Food: Meals and snacks lunchtimes only, 'till 2pm (2.30pm on Sat). Includes traditional Sunday roast.

General: Welcoming and comfortable pub overlooking the river near the town centre. It has an attractive and richly-decorated main room, with various alcoves and a snug-like fireside area at the end of the bar, plus a separate room. There's a raised platform by the darts board, which also serves as the stage for the jazz players in the town's annual festival. An open stove fire is due to be installed. Families and dogs welcome; popular with walkers.

PEAK FOREST - Derbyshire

Although its name derives from the medieval Royal Forest of the Peak, where nobles once hunted deer and boar, don't expect many trees. Instead, this village straddling the main road across the moors has a more recent and very curious claim to fame. In the early 18th century Peak Forest was Derbyshire's equivalent of Gretna Green, where runaway couples would be hastily wed by a local minister glorying in the title of 'Principal Official and Judge in Spiritualities in the Peculiar Court of Peak Forest'. It took an Act of Par-

North

liament in 1753 to halt the practice, and the former chapel has since been replaced. **Access:** 5 miles north east of Buxton (on A623).

Devonshire Arms

Peak Forest. Tel (01298) 23875
www.devarms.com
Grid ref: 114793
Open: 12-3, 6-11; 12-10.30 Sun.
Beer: Theakston's Best Bitter; John Smith's Bitter.
Food: Extensive and varied range of meals and snacks served lunchtime and evening till 9.30pm (all day till 9.30pm on Sunday) in bars or no-smoking dining area. Set menu, or changing specials that include roasted poussin stuffed with sage and onion, oven-roasted Gressingham Duck served on a bed of spinach purée, and tropical (vegetarian) curry.
Accommodation: 5 en-suite doubles (can include one twin).
General: Yet another Devonshire Arms (see mainly Central/East section for the Chatsworth connection!) this 17th century inn used to be one of six pubs or alehouses in the village, and was once called the Stag's Head – presumably a reference to the former royal hunting forest. Recent refurbishment has blended old and new, creating a more open plan feel, but the dining area remains pleasantly cosy. Families welcome (no children after 9pm), as are dogs and their owners. Small beer garden at rear.

> *Grog: spirits mixed with water, and named after the 'grogram coat' worn by Admiral Vernon (who insisted that sailors dilute their spirits)*

ROWARTH - Derbyshire

This out of the way village is reached down a cul-de-sac lane from the New Mills-Marple Bridge back road, and was once home to six cotton mills. However, by the early 20th century all its industry had ceased, and a terrible flood in 1930 wrecked what mill equipment was left, including the original water wheel at Little Mill. **Access:** 2 miles north of New Mills.

Little Mill Inn, Rowarth

Little Mill Inn

Rowarth. Tel (01663) 743178/746305
Grid ref: 011889
Open: 11-11; 12-10.30 Sun.
Beer: Camererons Strongarm; Banks's Bitter; Marston's Pedigree, plus one guest beer.
Food: Hot and cold food served in bar all day (until 10pm), including midweek specials, or separate menu with daily specials board in upstairs no-smoking restaurant (last orders 9pm), including the weekend carvery.
Accommodation: 2 self-catering cottages, plus three B&B double rooms in former Pullman railway carriage.
General: Fascinating old mill building full of character, featuring spacious open-plan bar complete with resident parrot, pool room, real fire and adjoining room incorporating old railway carriage seats and tables. Live bands every Wed (summer) and Fri, while outside there's terrace seating opposite the restored 36ft water wheel, plus a children's adventure playground across the lane. Families and dogs welcome inside and out.

SNAKE PASS - Derbyshire

The famous Snake Pass, which crosses the bleak and inhospitable moors of the Dark Peak (1,680 feet at its highest point), was engineered by Thomas Telford in the early 19th century. Its name derives from the Duke of Devonshire who petitioned parliament to allow the opening of a new Manchester-Sheffield route (his family crest features a snake). The pub is on the eastern (Bamford) side of the Pass - the modern A57 - about four miles from the far end of Ladybower Reservoir.

Snake Pass Inn

Ashopton Woodlands (A57).
Tel (01433) 651480
Grid ref: 113906
Open: 11-11; 12-10.30 Sun.

Beer: Four changing cask beers, such as Theakston's Best Bitter; Charles Wells Bombardier; Moorhouses Premier Bitter.

Food: Breakfast served 7.30-11am, then meals and snacks from 12-10pm. Choose from the varied menu - from ciabbata-style all day breakfast and the lunchtime Ramblers Platter through to steaks and specialities such as darne of salmon asparagus. Served in back bar (no smoking), hiker's bar or restaurant.

Accommodation: B&B - 5 en-suite doubles (1 family, 1 twin, 3 doubles, include two 4-posters), and camping barn at side.

General: The isolated inn was built as a half-way staging post for travellers, or rather more for their exhausted teams of horses. Today the new owners have plans to once more rejuvenate the place: besides the existing adventure playground a new childrens' nature trail is planned on the land behind the pub; live music nights (mainly jazz) have started; and most intriguingly of all building work has begun on a small indoor swimming pool, fitness suite, jacuzzi and outdoor hot tub – which will be open for residents and visitors alike. (After a long day on the hills what better way to relax?)

SPARROWPIT - Derbyshire

A tiny upland community by the Castleton junction of the A623 Chapel-en-le-Frith road. The pub sits on a tight hilltop bend with views over the exposed and rather sombre landscape.

Access: 5 miles north of Buxton (on A623).

Wanted Inn

Sparrowpit. Tel (01298) 812862
Grid ref: 092807
Open: 12-3, 5.30-11; 12-3, 5.30-10.30 Sun.

Beer: Robinson's Best Bitter, Hatters Mild, Fredericks, Young Tom or Hartleys XB.

Food: Appetising menu of sandwiches and light snacks through to decent-size hot meals, including a children's menu and

specific deals for OAPs. Changing specials board includes the likes of pan fried swordfish, griddled duck with bordelaise sauce, and haunch of lamb. Served in main bar or no-smoking dining area, 'till 9pm in evening.

General: This high and rather remote inn (c1700) on the route of the old saltway between Macclesfield and Castleton was originally called the 'Three Tuns', then in 1839 it became the Devonshire Arms. But when the pub came up for sale in 1956 and two years went by without a single bid it was renamed the Wanted Inn ('the pub that nobody wanted...'). Today its flagged floors and hearty meals attract walkers and potholers (nearby is Eldon Hole, the largest natural pothole in the Peak District). Families welcome, as are dogs, and there is a small outside seating area to the rear (the village playground is next door).

Devonshire Arms (now Wanted Inn), Sparrowpit (c.1947)

STONEY MIDDLETON - Derbyshire

'Stoney' is a small community huddled at the eastern end of the chasm of Middleton Dale which suffers, it has to be said, from the horrendously busy main road that splits it in two. It's believed that the village once sported a Roman bath (the thermal spring still exists), and nearby is the odd, octagonal church, built by Joan Padley in the 15th century after her husband's safe return from the Battle of Agincourt.

Access: 4 miles north of Bakewell (on A623).

"Claret is the liquor for boys; port for men; but he who aspires to be a hero must drink brandy." Samuel Johnson

North

Moon Inn

Stoney Middleton. Tel (01433) 630203
Grid ref: 232754
Open: 12-3, 6-11; 11-11 Sat; 12-10.30 Sun.
Beer: Stones Bitter, plus up to three guest beers such as Whim Hartington Bitter; Morland Old Speckled Hen; Wentworth Gryphon.
Food: Standard range of grills, steaks and fish dishes, with daily specials, plus sandwiches and light snacks. Served in either of two bars (one no-smoking) lunchtime and evening 'till 9pm; no food on Sun evening.
General: Heavily refurbished, two-bar pub at the foot of the village on the main road, it has a beer garden at the back. Walkers, families and dogs welcome.

STRINES - South Yorkshire

The pub sits in a delightfully peaceful location, alone on the hillside above Strines Reservoir - despite the western edge of Sheffield being little more than four miles away.
Access: Follow signs north off A57, between Ladybower and Sheffield.

Strines Inn

Bradfield Dale, Strines.
Tel (0114) 2851247
Grid ref: 223906
Open: 11-3, 7-11 (11-11 summer);
11-11 Sat; 12-10.30 Sun.
Beer: Two beers, which may include Mansfield Bitter; Marston's Pedigree; Camerons Strongarm.
Food: Menu ranges from six vegetarian options to local sausages and meat dishes, as well as light snacks and sandwiches. Look out in particular for the giant Yorkshire pudding (choice of meat and vegetarian). Served all day at weekends, lunchtime and evening during the week (till 9pm). One room no-smoking.
Accommodation: B&B - 3 rooms each with 4-poster beds, real fires or stoves, and breakfast served in rooms.
General: This handsome, remote building was originally a 13th century manor house, then renovated in the 1550s and opened as an inn in 1771. For a while it was known as the Tailor's Arms and served the

local turn-pike. Today it's a popular haunt of walkers, cyclists and the weekend set, who arrive in sometimes large numbers to enjoy its dark and atmospheric rooms decorated with stuffed animals, copper pots and all manner of curios. Outside there is extensive seating, as well as a children's adventure playground and animal farm. The pub is also noteworthy for blending its own coffee - it's won an award for Coffee Pub of the Year!

> **The Beer Prayer:**
> *Our lager*
> *Which art in barrels.*
> *Hallowed be thy drink.*
> *Thy will be drunk,*
> *At home as in tavern.*
> *Give us this day our foamy head,*
> *And forgive those who spill against us.*
> *And lead us not into incarceration,*
> *But deliver us from alcopops.*
> *For thine is the beer, the ale and the lager,*
> *Forever and ever,*
> *Barmen.*

Last Orders - pubs that are no more

Of all the pubs that have vanished in the Northern area few can have been oblit-erated with such finality as the Ashopton Inn, north of **Bamford**. The entire vil-lage of **Ashopton**, including the pub and the stately Derwent Hall, was demol-ished in 1943 so that the upper Derwent valley could be flooded to create the huge Ladybower Reservoir. Bamford itself lost the Rising Sun Hotel, sold off in 1967; and during 2001 the Marquis of Granby was closed. A few months before this happened the Hathersage Inn (formerly the Ordnance Arms Hotel) in the centre of **Hathersage** ceased trading as a traditional public house. Nearby, on Church Bank, the Blue Bell or Bell Inn disappeared around 1914/15, and **Bradwell's** Valley Lodge looks likely to join the Newburgh Arms as an ex-pub. Further down the Derwent the three current hostelries in **Calver** were once sup-plemented by a further five pubs or alehouses (the Miner's Arms, Bull's Head, London Tavern, Silent Woman, and the Drum and Monkey). In **Eyam** the Bull's Head, which stood opposite the church and was once called the Talbot Inn, was replaced with private apartments in the late 1990s. At **Hope** the list of former pubs includes the Blacksmiths Arms, which was later renamed the Horse Shoe, the Cross Daggers and the Durham Ox, which later became the village post office. Perhaps the most unusual location was enjoyed by customers of the for-mer Peak Cavern Inn at **Castleton**. Until the late 1700s it could be found inside the actual entrance of the cavern, together with several other cottages inhabited by ropemakers. The damp air at the cavern entrance was ideal for their craft.

It is said that there were as many as 16 pubs or beerhouses in **Hayfield**, in the north-west of the area, and although **Glossop** still boasts a large number of drinking holes several have departed (or rather have been converted into restau-rants) recently, including the Whiteley Nab and the Lamp; and in Old Glossop the Hare and Hounds, Ring o'Bells and the Greyhound are all long gone. At remote **Crowden**, situated by Torside Reservoir in the bleak Pennine valley of Longdendale, the Commercial Inn survived until the 1920s when it was pulled down. A similar fate befell the George and Dragon, which for over 300 years stood at the nearby Holmfirth turning and was closed in 1961 because Manchester Corporation deemed it too near their valuable reservoir water. A mile up that road (by Heyden Bridge) there once stood the Tollemarche Arms — but depending on your poison you could be in for a shock since it was a temperance inn! Heading eastwards, the now deserted village of **Woodhead**, which clustered above the station next to the tunnel entrance, used to sport the Angel Inn until the 1920s. Nearing the top of the Woodhead Pass, the former hamlet of **Saltersbrook** once included the Millers Arms (closed 1913), while at the summit the Plough and Farrow (which later became Fiddlers Green) disappeared half a century before. Today all that remains are just a few forlorn stones amid the des-olate moorland.

Part Three: Western Area

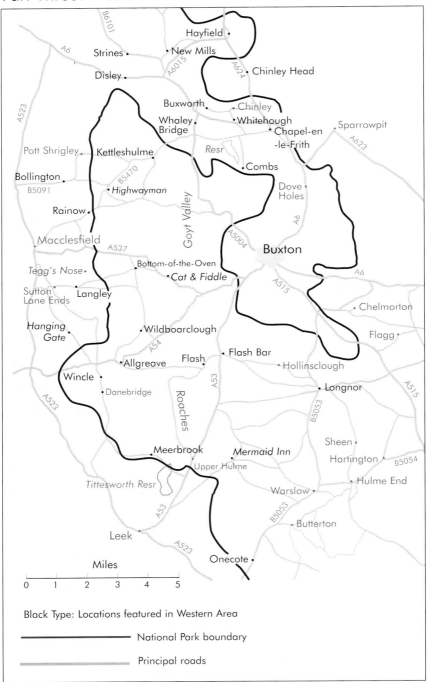

Hayfield •
Strines • • New Mills
Disley • • Chinley Head
B6101
A6
A6015
A624
A523

Buxworth •
Whaley • • Chinley
Bridge • • Whitehough
Sparrowpit •
Pott Shrigley • Kettleshulme • Chapel-en
-le-Frith
A623
Bollington • *Resr*
B5091 • Combs
B5470
Highwayman Dove
Holes •
Rainow • Goyt Valley A6
A5004

Macclesfield A5004
A537 Buxton
Bottom-of-the-Oven • A515
Tegg's Nose • • *Cat & Fiddle*
Sutton Chelmorton •
Lane Ends • Langley
Flagg •
Hanging • Wildboarclough
Gate A54
Wincle Flash • Flash Bar Hollinsclough •
• Allgreave A53 • Longnor
A523 • Danebridge B5053
A515
Roaches Sheen •
• Meerbrook • *Mermaid Inn* Hartington • B5054
Tittesworth Resr Upper Hulme • Hulme End
Warslow •
A53 B5053
Leek • Butterton •
A523 Onecote •

Miles
0   1   2   3   4   5

Black Type: Locations featured in Western Area

———————— National Park boundary

———————— Principal roads

ALLGREAVE - Cheshire

Located on the A54 six miles south-west of Buxton near the turning for Wincle.

Rose and Crown

Allgreave. Tel (01260) 227232
Grid ref: 974670
Open: 12-3, 7-11; (occasionaly 11-11 Sat);
12-3, 7-10.30 Sun (occasionally 12-10.30 Sun).
Beer: Robinson's Best Bitter, and one Robinson's seasonal beer.
Food: Inviting choice of main menu (local Danebridge trout, dusted lime and coriander salmon, super hot chicken curry), bar snacks, or separate and highly original vegetarian blackboard - Szechuan vegetables, Borlotti bean goulash, Singapore noodles, etc. Served in bar or no-smoking dining room from 12-2.30, 7-9.
Accommodation: B&B - 2 double, 1 twin, all en-suite.
General: This friendly hillside pub is a long, narrow building that inside is a bit mixed-up but full of character. At the far end the function room used to house a smithy; next is the comfortable lounge bar with open fire; then beyond the narrow bar with wooden pew, rocking chair and fish tank, is the new-looking dining room with views over the valley below. Families and dogs welcome; garden set into the hillside to the rear.

BOLLINGTON - Cheshire

There are apparently up to 19 pubs and clubs in and around this fairly small Cheshire town! Just to the south is a prominent ridge (Kerridge Hill) topped by a curious whitewashed monument known as White Nancy, reachable by public footpath. The two pubs included here are both at the far eastern end of Bollington.
Access: Around 3 miles from Macclesfield on the B5091, on the very western edge of the Peak District.

Church House Inn

Church Street. Tel (01625) 574014
Grid ref: 939778
Open: 12-3, 5.30-11; 12-3, 6-10.30 Sun.
Beer: Jennings Cumberland Ale; Greene King IPA, plus one guest beer, such as Courage Directors; Timothy Taylor's Landlord; Theakston's XB.
Food: Set menu and daily specials board, including sandwiches and snacks, plus a range of home-made pies (prime steak and onion, lamb and redcurrant), minty lamb casserole, fish, and so on. Served throughout pub, including no-smoking room, 12-2, 6.30-9.30 (9pm on Sun).
Accommodation: 5 en-suite rooms (3 single, 1 family, 1 double).
General: Well-presented back street pub, probably knocked through from a couple of terraced houses. Clean, tidy and friendly, with one open bar, plus no-smoking room and extra seating upstairs. The two log fires give the bar a warm and cosy feel, and look out for the ivy growing through the skylight in the Gents! Families welcome; some outside seating by car park at rear.

Poachers Inn

95 Ingersley Road. Tel (01625) 572086
www.thepoachersinnbollington.co.uk
Grid ref: 944778
Open: 12-2.30, 5.30-11; 12-2.30, 7-10.30 Sun.
Beer: Boddington's Bitter; Timothy Taylor's Landlord, plus two guest beers, which may include local selections from the Coach House Brewing Company of Warrington, and Storm Brewing of Macclesfield.
Food: Well-priced two-course lunch Mon-Fri (including home-made soups like spicy parsnip and carrot and coriander); and evenings 5.30-9.45 (from 7pm at weekends). Bar food also available weekdays, otherwise it's à la carte in the no-smoking Gamekeeper Restaurant where choices include the likes of sea bass, ostrich fillets and wild mushroom medley. Bookings advisable for weekends.
General: 200 year old former mill cottages on the very edge of town, the pub used to be called the Masonic, but now as the Poachers it is a comfortable and popular place and furnished with all manner of curios, prints and pictures, sets of antlers, and so on. To the rear is a very pleasant and secluded garden. Children welcome if eating; no dogs. The regular theme nights sound like fun: Chinese Banquet, Italian Evening, Indian Night and Mexican Fiestas.

Pub's closure provides a cautionary tale

A mile to the north of Bollington is a small village with the delightful name of Pott Shrigley, but the demise of its pub early last century is evidence if needed of the dire consequences of over-imbibing on the Sabbath. The Lowther Arms was named after the Lord of the Manor, and by all accounts was a pleasant village inn. But one particular Sunday morning in 1922 as Lady Constance Lowther was emerging from church she detected alcohol on the breath of her groom, and in a fit of moral rage promptly closed the village pub for good. However, there is a far more indecent version of this story (preferred by most locals, it has to be said) which has Lady Constance catching her groom relieving himself against the wheels of her carriage. (As a matter of interest it is still legal in Britain to urinate against the offside rear wheel of a taxi! The driver won't see it this way and it's probably safer not to try.)

BOTTOM-OF-THE-OVEN - Cheshire

An out-of-the-way, valley bottom location to the east of the Macclesfield Forest/Tegg's Nose, with good views up to the Cat and Fiddle, and south towards Shutlingsloe. The curious name is thought to derive from a large oven or spit roast that was once a feature of nearby Oven Lane, and which fed the men of Lord Stanley of Crag Hall (at Wildboarclough) - hence the name of both the pub and its location.

Access: 4 miles west of Buxton (off A537).

Stanley Arms

Bottom-of-the-Oven, Macclesfield Forest.
Tel (01260) 252414
Grid ref: 981724
Open: 12-3, 5.30-11; Sat 11-11; 12-10.30 Sun.
Beer: Marston's Bitter, Pedigree, plus one guest beer.
Food: Range of appetising hot and cold home-cooked food, with lunchtime menu including warm baguettes, cottage pie, black pudding and chops, and more adventurous à la carte evening menu fea-turing dishes such as of shark, guinea fowl and the ever-popular Bottom-of-the-Oven lamb. Served in bars (one no-smoking) or separate no-smoking dining room, Mon-Fri 12-2.30, 5.30-9 (9.30 Fri), all day Sat 'till 9.30 and Sun 'till 8pm.
General: Attractive, isolated stone building, set at the foot of plunging hillside that makes it a popular venue for walkers. Inside the pub is full of character, with the three small and elegant rooms featuring period fireplaces and little modern pub clutter. The smart dining room is equally refined, enjoying some good views across the valley. Children welcome 'till 8.30pm (separate room at back), and dogs in large porch only. Singer performs every third Friday of the month; beer garden to rear and benches at front.

Short measured - and short changed

When you pay for a pint of beer you should get just that: a whole pint. If you receive an inch of froth on your beer this is a short measure, and you should politely ask for it to be topped up. Some pubs serve beer in oversized glasses to allow for 'the head', with the pint mark clearly shown, but always check and if you're not sure then ask. If you are still not happy with the service you receive then report the pub to the nearest trading standards office, details of which can be found at local town halls, and at www.tradingstandards.co.uk. Of course it is traditional for many northern beers to have a head, just as it is for some southern beers to have virtually no head at all. But if you pay for a pint of beer then surely you should expect to be served a pint of beer? Well apparently not, since recent Government proposals suggested that while an average pint of beer should ideally constitute 100% liquid it should certainly be "no less than 95% liquid". In effect this means that if you pay £2.00 for a pint of beer you are liable to be throwing away 10p each time! Would you be happy to be short-changed like this on a litre of petrol, or a pint of milk? No - so if you pay for a pint of beer then ask for exactly that.

BUXTON - Derbyshire

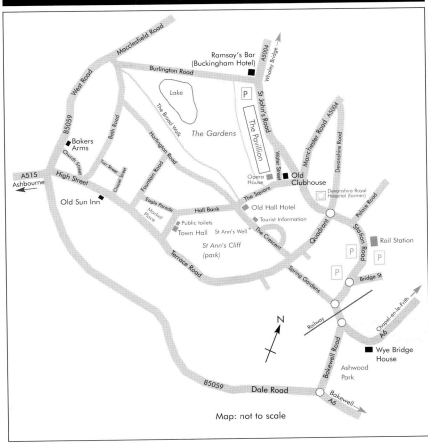

Map: not to scale

The Romans were the first to make use of the thermal springs that lie beneath this high Derbyshire town. They called it Aqvae Arnemetiae (the Spa of the Goddess of the Grove), and ever since then visitors have journeyed to Buxton to sample the waters that maintain a constant temperature of 28°C (82°F). An unceasing stream of pure if tepid drinking water issues out of St Anne's Well, on The Crescent, and is bottled daily by local residents and intrepid visitors - indeed the author's continuing good health is a testimony to this rich source. The recently-restored Crescent (designed by John Carr of York) is one of a number of impressive pieces of architecture that can

be found in the central area of town. Other must-sees are the Opera House, a grand Edwardian building which holds regular live events including the annual Gilbert and Sullivan Festival; the Devonshire Royal Hospital, with its massive unsupported dome, that is set to be part of the University of Derby's new Buxton campus; and the handsome Pavilion Gardens, complete with lakes, lawns and footbridges over the canalised River Wye. More details from Buxton Tourist Information Centre on The Crescent, tel (01298) 25106. Buxton was intended to be the spa town of the north, a rival to Bath, but at 1,000 ft high it's often a touch nippy and frequently experiences rain or snow when the likes of Bakewell or Matlock are dry. In such an event head for one of Buxton's many pubs - there are at least 20 to keep you occupied, and those listed below are merely a cross-section of the best or more original.

Bakers Arms

26 West Road. Tel (01298) 24404
www.communities.msn.com/bakersarmsbuxton
Grid ref: 057729
Open: 12-2 (closed Fri, Sat lunch), 6(4 Tue)-11; 12-3, 6-10.30 Sun.

Beer: Greene King Abbot Ale; Tetley Bitter; Kelham Island (Best, Pale or Easy Rider), and one guest beer.

General: Small but handsome old pub off the main road, originally believed to have been a bakers. The two small bars are tidy and comfortable, and furnished with an array of football memorabilia, including some fascinating old photos, and mementoes from the pub's team's overseas tours. Live music each Sunday, usually an Irish duo. Some benches by pavement out the front. No children or dogs inside.

Old Clubhouse

1 Water Street. Tel (01298) 70117
Grid ref: 056736
Open: 11-11; 12-10.30 Sun.

Beer: Tetley Bitter; Inde Coope Burton Ale, plus a seasonal summer beer.

Food: Served all day till approx 9pm, in large bar or no-smoking dining room. Choice of lunchtime snacks, hot and old sandwiches, or main meals ('pots and pies') and daily specials.

General: Built in 1822 and originally a gentlemen's club, this large and elegant establishment opposite the Opera House is popular with evening concert-goers, and during the Buxton Festival each summer the road outside is closed for mingling and socialising. With its high-ceilings, large bay windows, and the inevitable theatre memorabilia, the place has plenty of character, if not exactly intimacy. Families welcome; no dogs. Small area of garden seating to the side.

> *"One more drink and I'll be under the host."*
> Dorothy Parker

Old Sun Inn

33 High Street. Tel (01298) 23452
Grid ref: 057732
Open: 11-11; !2-10.30 Sun.

Beer: Marston's Bitter, Pedigree; Banks's Bitter; Cameron's Strong Arm, plus one guest beer.

Food: Served 12-2.30, 5,30-9 Mon-Fri, and 12-9 at weekends. Eat in bar or no-smoking dining room. Bar menu includes lamb creole, liver and onions, sirloin steak and stilton, plus vegetarian choices and a changing specials board.

General: Located on the High Street (A515 to Ashbourne) beyond the hilltop market place, in what the map calls Higher Buxton. Considerably but carefully refurbished, this large old pub is a rabbit warren of small dark rooms and cosy alcoves, partitions and snugs. The stripped wood or tiled floors, mix of old furniture and voluminous settees give the place a relaxed feel, although it can get busy at weekends. Wheelchair access from car park at rear, and disabled toilet. Children welcome until 9pm. No dogs inside, but picnic tables back from roadside at the front.

Ramsay's Bar (Buckingham Hotel)

Burlington Road. Tel (01298) 70481
Grid ref: 054734
Open: 12-2.30/3, 6-11 (10.30 Sun).

Beer: Usually as many as six real ales available - Timothy Taylor's Landlord and Charles Wells Bombardier, plus three to four guest beers.

Food: Choice of bar food menu (includes grills, pasta, toasted sandwiches, etc) served 12-2, 6.15-9.15/9.30, and no-smoking restaurant and carvery 7.30-9/9.15pm daily (steaks, fresh fish, vegetarian, etc, plus Ice Cream Sundae or Sorbet of the Day).

Accommodation: 39 hotel rooms (mixed).

General: Built in 1876/7 as two houses and overlooking the western end of the Pavilion Gardens, this elegant hotel opened in the early 1900s and has been welcoming a steady stream of guests ever since, not least because of its good food and impressive range of real ales. Ramsay's

Bar, which is long and comfortable and contains numerous pictures of stars of stage and screen, is open to non-residents and named after the artist George Ramsay who once lived here. Families, dogs welcome; wheelchair access and facilities currently being upgraded. A few outside tables.

Wye Bridge House

Fairfield Road. Tel (01298) 70932
Grid ref: 064737
Open: 11-11; 12-10.30 Sun.
Beer: Greene King Abbot Ale; Theakston's Best Bitter; Shepherd Neame Spitfire; Hop Back Summer Lightning; Marston's Pedigree, plus several guest beers.
Food: Served all day until 10pm throughout the pub, including a sizeable no-smoking area. Standard Wetherspoons menu, including curry club, steaks, baps and light bites, plus special deals.
General: This large and quite imposing Wetherspoons pub to the east of the town centre is located beyond the railway viaduct, on the A6 (Fairfield Road) towards Manchester. Spacious and airy, its modern and open-plan design allows plenty of standing room, and there's an area of outside seating overlooking an attractive riverside park. Disabled toilet and ramp. Usual Wetherspoons range of events, including beer festivals. Children allowed if eating ('till 6pm). No dogs inside.

> *"Once, during prohibition, I was forced to live on nothing but food and water."*
>
> *W.C.Fields*

BUXWORTH - Derbyshire

This small settlement clustered around the open, leafy basin of the Peak Forest Canal was originally known as Bugsworth, but locals decided to change the name in 1929 (although confusingly the canal basin is still usually called Bugsworth Basin). It remains unique as the country's only canal-tramway interchange, and was where quarried limestone was brought down from Dove Holes on the part-gravity-fed Peak Forest Tramway to be loaded on to the canal boats before heading off for Manchester and the Macclesfield Canal. It fell into disuse in the 1920s, but recent restoration work aims to bring this fascinating place back to life.
Access: One mile north-west of Whaley Bridge (off A6).

Navigation Inn

Bugsworth Canal Basin. Tel (01663) 732072
www.navigationinn.co.uk
Grid ref: 023821
Open: 11-11; 12-10.30 Sun.
Beer: Timothy Taylor's Landlord ; Marston's Pedigree; Webster's Yorkshire Bitter, plus one guest beer.
Food: Coffee is served from mid morning and food every lunchtime and evening 'till 9pm (all day at weekends), throughout the bars or in the separate Odessa Restaurant. Set menu includes roasts and grills, fish of the day, plus daily changing specials board, as well as a 'Minnows Menu' for children under 10.
Accommodation: B&B - 6 en-suite rooms (2 family, 2 doubles, 1 single) and 1 twin, non en-suite.
General: This long, narrow brick building has overlooked the canal basin for 200 years, and inside it's like a shrine to a bygone age: prints, books and canal memorabilia are scattered throughout, and in the cosy snug with its wood-burning stove you can watch videos detailing the life and times of the canal and its trade. Outside terraced seating. Families welcome; dogs allowed in bar area.

> *Dantzic Spruce: 'The most famous spruce beer, made from essence of the green buds of the black spruce fir, dissolved in a strong syrup to which yeast and spice are added'*
> (from The Pickwick Papers by Charles Dickens)

CAT AND FIDDLE - Cheshire

A famous location high on the Peak District's bleak western moorland, and the point at which the busy Buxton-Macclesfield road finally struggles to the summit and gazes into Cheshire one side and Derbyshire the other. One of the most remote and exposed pubs in England, its height of 1,690 feet also makes it the second highest, behind the Tan Hill Inn in the North Pennines .
Access: 3 miles west of Buxton (A537).

What's in a (pub) name?

Most of the pub names in the Peak District are fairly straightforward and reflect obvious themes like work and pastimes (Miner's Arms, Wheatsheaf, Packhorse Inn, Sportsman, Angler's Rest), or are named after local well-to-do local families (Rutland Arms, Devonshire Arms) and monarchs (King's Head, Red Lion, Crown, etc). Thankfully the recent and largely urban trend of renaming pubs with wacky and supposedly humorous names (eg the Snooty Fox or Brahms and Lizt) has not permeated the region, although you could be forgiven for thinking that the otherwise splendid Waltzing Weasel at Birch Vale, near New Mills, had succumbed. In fact the name was altered as far back as 1965, and when asked by the local justices for her reason for the change the then landlady replied: "It sounds more rural in character, it has scientific foundation, and it's a far more entertaining title than the present 'Birch Hall Inn'!" The Cat and Fiddle's name is also well-established, so much so that drivers, walkers and even map-makers refer to the location by the pub's name. The origin would seem to be the much-loved nursery rhyme ("Hey diddle diddle, the cat and the fiddle"), although one account suggests that the name was introduced in 1857 after the Duke of Devonshire presented the landlord with a picture of a cat playing a violin - see the sculptured relief by the main porch. But another intriguing possibility is that it stretches back to the Middle Ages and has some connection with Caton de Fidele, the governor of the English-held town of Calais. Mind you, isn't a breezy Cheshire moorland somewhat far removed from the English Channel?

Cat and Fiddle

Buxton Road (A537), Cat and Fiddle.
Tel (01298) 23364
Grid ref: 002719
Open: 11-11; 12-10.30 Sun.
Beer: Robinson's Best Bitter, Old Stockport Bitter, plus a third beer from Robinsons.
Food: Wide-ranging menu served in either bar or largely no-smoking dining room from 11-8.30 Mon-Sat, 12-8.30 Sun. Due to the altitude and exposed position of the pub it's not surprising that most popular are the hot meals such as roasts, hot-pots, home-made chilli and filled Yorkshire puddings.
General: Given its isolated, hilltop position, the pub is inevitably sturdy rather than attractive, built to withstand the winter gales. The Moorland Bar is specifically for walkers, bikers and dog-owners, while the cosier lounge bar is open and well-heated, leading off to the dining area. A new wheelchair ramp has just been built, and disabled toilets are already installed. Families very welcome; occasional live music. Tends to get very busy on summer weekends and bank holidays.

CHAPEL-EN-LE-FRITH - Derbyshire

Five miles north of Buxton is the small town of Chapel-en-le-Frith, which like Whaley Bridge is these days a thankfully much more peaceful place due to the A6 bypass. Its name means chapel in the forest, and dates from a chapel built here in 1225 in honour of the lately-murdered Thomas a Beckett in Canterbury Cathedral (the 14th century parish church was built on the site of the original chapel). No doubt he would be surprised to learn that these days the town revolves around Ferodo brake linings, which is the main local employer. By and large it's a quiet and handy, if rather unexciting, centre from which to explore the High Peak.

Hanging Gate

Manchester Road (B5470). Tel (01298) 812776
Grid ref: 042799
Open: 11-11; 12-10.30 Sun.
Beer: Theakston's Best Bitter.
Food: Hot and cold meals served all day - from breakfast at 8am through till 10pm. Full range on offer, from children's and senior citizens' meals to business lunches and family outings. Food served in bar or dining area (no smoking).
General: Situated a mile west of Chapel on the B5470, this large dining pub is very popular with families, offering full disabled access and toilets, mother and baby facili-

ties, and an adventure playground outside by the car park. Fenced beer garden also available. Although modernised inside, the older features of the tavern by the once-busy toll gate mostly remain. However, OS maps still refers to this area as Cockyard, and apparently the unsavoury spectacle of cock fighting once took place in a pit behind the pub.

> *Cold Tankard: a drink comprising perry (or cider or ale), lemon rind, brandy and sugar*

King's Arms Hotel

Market Place. Tel (01298) 812105
Grid ref: 056807
Open: 11-11; 12-10.30 Sun.
Beer: Tetley Bitter; Boddingtons Bitter; Greenalls Bitter.
Food: Lunchtime meals only (12-2), in bar or no-smoking dining room by prior arrangement. The menu features dishes such as bangers and mash, bubble and squeak, doorstep sandwiches and hot breadcakes with various fillings.
Accommodation: B&B - 10 mixed rooms (some en-suite).
General: Overlooking the main market place, this imposing and historic hotel retains some of its former glories, most notably in the elegant oak-panelled dining room. The single, open bar has been refurbished by the Porter's Ale House chain, the current owners, and in the evenings the wide-screen TV and weekly live music (bands and soloists) can make it a busy place. No dogs inside, but families welcome.

Roebuck Inn

9 Market Place. Tel (01298) 812274
Grid ref: 056807
Open: 11-11; 12-10.30 Sun.
Beer: Courage Directors; Tetley Bitter, Mild, plus usually one guest beer.
Food: Snacks and specials (sandwiches through to roasts) served lunchtimes only: 12-2 Mon-Sat, 12-4 Sun. Evening meals by prior arrangement only.
General: Chapel's traditional market pub, which before all-day opening arrived was the only place allowed to stay open at exceptional times for the traders. It remains a handsome, engaging place, where you

meet to drink and talk. Families are welcome, as are dogs (and, according to a sign, cats!). Apart from a small games room to the rear, it's an open-plan building, traditionally and tastefully-decorated with plenty of tables and an open fire by the bar.

Royal Oak

Market Street. Tel (01298) 814671
Grid ref: 055806
Open: 11-11; 12-10.30 Sun.
Beer: Burtonwood Bitter.
Food: Quality range of food served 12-2.30, 5-10 Mon-Sat, and all day 'till 10pm on Sun. Eat in bar or separate dining area; no-smoking section. Choose from mouth-watering specials board or extensive set menu, which includes some rather unusual dishes - agubzuf pancakes (broccoli and cheese), renbold chicken (named after local builders), and Whaley fish 'big, bold and battered.' Children's portions available; booking advisable for weekends.
Accommodation: B&B - 7 rooms (4 doubles/singles, 3 twin).
General: On the main street opposite the market place, this large pub was apparently once the town's courthouse. Today it's refurbished and very comfortable, with a knocked-through series of rooms incorporating a pleasant dining area. At the rear is a quiet patio with tables, overlooking the bowling green. No children after 9pm.

CHINLEY HEAD - Derbyshire

Located between Whaley Bridge and Chapel-en-le-Frith, on the B6062, and perhaps best-known for a series of impressive Victorian viaducts that still carry commuters into Manchester.

Lamb Inn

Hayfield Road (A624). Tel (01663) 750519
Grid ref: 049844
Open: 11.30-3, 6-11; 12-3, 6-10.30 Sun.
Beer: Bass.
Food: Features over 60s lunch menu and all-day Sunday roast, and the specials board includes the likes of spicy stir fried king prawns, lamb and mint suet pudding and hanky panky ice cream pie. Served throughout the pub 12-2.30, 6-9.30, and

West

all day weekends until 10pm (Sat) and 9.30pm (Sun). Some no-smoking areas - (NB pipe smoking is forbidden in all areas!) **General:** This popular family eating pub is to be found 1 $^1/_2$ miles north of Chinley on the Hayfield Road near Chinley Head. It was originally three separate quarrymen's cottages, built in 1769, but now it's a plush and comfortable series of small rooms that's often busy with diners (booking advisable at peak times). Families and walkers welcome; seating area outside.

COMBS - Derbyshire

Combs (pronounced 'Coombs') is an out of the way sort of place, a sleepy and rather disjointed village on a lane that doesn't go anywhere below some big hills that very few people walk. Nearby Combs Reservoir is a popular destination for trout fishermen. **Access:** 2 miles south-west of Chapel-en-le-Frith (off B5470).

Beehive

Combs. Tel (01298) 812758
Grid ref: 042786
Open: 6-11 (12-3, 6-11 Mon-Fri summer); 12-3, 6-11 (11-11 summer) Sat; 12-3, 6-10.30 (12-10.30 summer) Sun.
Beer: Black Sheep Best Bitter, plus one guest beer.
Food: Decent pub menu ranges from hot filled ciabattas to chef's curry of the day, imaginative vegetarian options (hazelnut roast, cannelloni provençale) and home-made ice cream and puddings. Served 12-2.30 (not Mon-Fri in winter) and 6-9; and all day 'till 9pm at weekends in peak season. Separate restaurant available, and sizeable section of main bar is no-smoking. **General:** A large, traditional stone-built building, with a light and spacious main bar that's graced with open fires and polished floorboards throughout. There's also a small tap room and dining room, and plans to develop accommodation in the long run. Outside seating in a walled area by the front. Families welcome; dogs in tap room only.

> *"I only drink to make other people seem more interesting."* George Jean Nathan

DISLEY - Cheshire

Despite the busy A6 and its proximity to Stockport, Disley has some attractive old buildings and is a handy centre from which to explore Lyme Park. The 1,400 acres of parkland and moor is today managed by the National Trust, and the network of paths and open spaces offer some fine views east towards the Kinder Scout massif. The centrepiece of the Country Park is a Palladian mansion complete with rose garden and orangery - it was used as Mr Darcy's house in the popular BBC's adaptation of Jane Austen's 'Pride and Prejudice'. Lyme Park is open all year round, and the House generally Apr-Oct.
Access: 2 miles west of New Mills.

> *For details of public transport connections in Greater Manchester call GMPTE on 0161 228 7811*

Dandy Cock

15 Market Street. Tel (01663) 763712
Grid ref: 976847
Open: 11-11; 12-10.30 Sun.
Beer: Robinson's Best, Hatter's Mild.
Food: Decent and well-priced range of hot and cold food served 12-9.30 daily in separate dining room (part no-smoking). From hot and cold sandwiches and jacket potatoes through to popular roast dinners and specials such as Cajun chicken and prawn and crab fishcakes. Children's menu, plus senior citizen's special (12-6).
General: Friendly and unassuming local on main street, comprising one small and cosy main bar with interesting prints of Disley over the years, plus an open fire and a separate, screened-off dining area. Welcomes walkers and families.

Ram's Head

Buxton Road West. Tel (01663) 767909
Grid ref: 974846
Open: 11-11; 12-10.30 Sun.
Beer: Bass; Tetleys Bitter.
Food: An extensive set menu, and specials board in season. Hot meals include the usual grills, roasts and vegetarian options, plus dishes such as sausage and mash, wild mushroom risotto, and mouth-watering wraps

(bacon & avocado, salmon & cream cheese). Varied wine list. Food served throughout the pub (much of which is no-smoking), 12-10 Mon-Sat, 12-9.30 Sun.

General: A large and handsome old coach-inn by the crossroads in the centre of Disley (look for the old mounting block outside). Comprehensively refurbished by Vintage Inns, the spacious and comfortable series of rooms are elegantly-decorated and well-lit, with three open log fires. At the back is a large and secluded area of patio and lawn seating, very popular in summer, plus two crown greens belonging to the pub at which patrons can try their hands at bowls! Full wheelchair access and toilets; families welcome; no dogs inside.

FLASH - Staffordshire

Billed as the highest village in England, at 1,518 feet above sea level, the small village of Flash can be a cold and windy location.

Access: 4 miles south of Buxton (off A53).

New Inn

Flash Tel (01298) 22941
Grid ref: 025673
12-2.30 (3 Sat), 6-11; 12-3; 6.10.30 Sun.
Beer: Bass.
Food: No meals, only occasional snacks such as oatcakes, pork pies, etc.
General: Originally a 17th century farm, it's a solid little inn that has maintained its character by shunning the bright lights and noise of too many modern pubs. There's no hot food, accommodation or music, but with a log fire lit most of the year it's a cosy and peaceful location appealing to older customers in particular. No small children, no dogs.

> *"There is nothing which has yet been contrived by man, by which so much happiness is produced as by a good tavern or inn."*
> Samuel Johnson

FLASH BAR - Staffordshire

Located half a mile north of Flash itself, on a bend of the A53 overlooking the huge rugged green spread of the Staffordshire Moorlands.

Traveller's Rest

Flash Bar (A53) Tel (01298) 23695
Grid ref: 033677
Open: 12-3 (closed Mon lunchtime), 6-11; 11-11 Sat; 12-10.30 Sun.
Beer: Tetley Bitter; Marston's Pedigree; Whim Hartington Bitter and usually two guest beers (such as Fuller's London Pride; Everards Tiger; Morland Old Speckled Hen). Also look out for Eliot's Spiced Mulled Wine on tap, and selection of malt whiskies.
Food: Large set menu and changing specials board, featuring hot and cold snacks and meals. Popular dishes include braised beef in Guinness, and tasty soups and pies (all made on the premises). Served every lunchtime (except Mon) and evening until 9pm throughout the pub, which includes a no-smoking area.
General: A sturdy 17th century inn perched on a remote and exposed hilltop on the Buxton-Leek road (A53), and which claims to be the third highest pub in England after Tan Hill Inn and the Cat and Fiddle. It once made the Guinness Book of Records for having 76 beer pumps on the bar, and serving 42 different brews! It's cosy and welcoming, with log fires at either end, and the long, open building is stuffed full of antiques and bizarre curios. Families welcome; dogs in bar area only. Live jazz every first Thurs of the month, plus other regular music nights.

KETTLESHULME - Cheshire

A small village 1 1/2 miles south-west of Whaley Bridge, on B5470.

Swan Inn

Macclesfield Road (B5470). Tel (01663) 732943
Grid ref: 987797
Open: 12-3, 5.30-11 Mon-Thu; 11-11 Fri, Sat; 12-10.30 Sun.
Beer: Thwaites Bitter, plus three guest beers (mostly from small breweries like Wye Valley, Whim, etc).
Food: Range of hot and cold food, from sandwiches to home-made soups and pies, served lunchtime only, 12-2.
General: Small and very attractive old pub, though whether it's 'XV century' as the sign outside suggests is open to ques-

tion. The dark and cosy interior sports huge beams, log fires, a grandfather clock and period seating. Dogs allowed inside, and children are welcome in the cosy Copper Room (decorated as you would imagine) or beer garden to the side of the building. Walkers also very welcome.

Swan Inn, Kettleshulme

LANGLEY - Cheshire

Neither pub is actually in the village of Langley, which is located at the very western edge of the Peak District near Macclesfield. The Leathers Smithy is just to the east of the village by Ridgegate Reservoir, with the dark green conifers of Macclesfield Forest extending beyond. Behind and above is the distinctive protuberance of Tegg's Nose (see separate feature). The Hanging Gate is 1¹/₂ miles south-east of Langley, on a high and panoramic lane between Sutton Lane Ends and the Danebridge/Wincle crossroads of the A54.
Access: From Macclesfield, leave the A523 (Leek road), taking a lane through Sutton Lane Ends to reach Langley.

Hanging Gate
Higher Sutton. Tel (01260) 252238
Grid ref: 963697
Open: 12-3, 7-11; 11-11 Sat; 12-10.30 Sun.
Beer: Hydes Bitter, Jekylls Gold, plus one Hydes seasonal beer.
Food: Quality range of food, from cod (in a home-made, speciality batter) and duck to spinach and basil lasagne, marinated herrings in dill and Thai crab cakes. Sunday roast, home-made puddings, plus large plate/small plate set meal choices.

Served 12-2, 7-9.30 Mon-Sat, 12-2 (only) Sun, in either of two small bars, no-smoking Blue Room and downstairs 'View Room' with panoramic views - but advance booking advisable, especially at weekends.
General: A real gem of a pub, situated high (almost 1,100 ft) on a ridge with breathtaking views across Cheshire. An inn since 1621, the two small, dark bars have open fires and ooze character. Next door is the tiny and dignified Blue Room, complete with a chaise longue, while downstairs the dining room enjoys great views over the valley. Naturally the outside seating is popular in summer, but families are welcome inside, and dogs in the snug only. The name reflects the building's location near the spot where poachers and rustlers caught in the Royal Macclesfield Forest were hanged.

Leathers Smithy
Clarke Lane. Tel (01260) 252313
Grid ref: 963715
Open: 12-3, 7-11; 11-11 Sat; 12-10.30 Sun.
Beer: Theakston's Best; Marston's Pedigree; Courage Directors, plus one guest beer.
Food: Decent range of home-made hot and cold food with a changing specials board that includes lime and coriander chicken kebab, aubergine stuffed with cous cous, marinated piri chicken. Served in bar or no-smoking dining room 12-2, 7-10 Mon-Fri, 12-10 Sat and 12-9 Sun.
General: This 18th century building was formerly a smithy and is named after William Leather, a local farrier who became the pub's first licensee in 1821. As you enter there's a small area to the right with a flagged floor and open fire, ideal for walkers, while to the left is a larger, plusher area for diners and drinkers. Children are welcome in the dining room to the rear, and there's a beer at the back. No dogs inside.

The gritstone hills

Tegg's Nose Country Park, above Langley, is based on an old gritstone quarry, which supplied building material for local villages and towns such as Langley and Macclesfield. There's now a small visitor centre by the main car park at the top, and from the exposed summit there are great views over the dense plantations of Macclesfield Forest, with their partly-hidden reservoirs, to the coned summit of Shutlingsloe (1,659 ft). However, the highest point in Cheshire is in fact Shining Tor (1,834 ft), away to the east. Tegg's Nose is also on the route of the Gritstone Trail, an 18-mile walking route that runs from Rushton Spencer in Staffs to Lyme Park near Disley. It traverses the gritstone hills and ridges of the Peak District's far western flanks, and offers a series of terrific views across the Cheshire Plain to the Irish Sea.

LONGNOR - Staffordshire

An interesting, once-thriving small town situated on a prominent ridge separating the Dove and Manifold valleys. The pubs are mostly gathered around the cobbled main square, where the Victorian market hall is now a craft centre, and off which is an art gallery and other shops (including a decent chippy). In bygone days this Staffordshire market town was a busy place, acting as a focus for the local farming community and surrounding cottage industries. It was also a stopover for wagons and traders moving between the Potteries, the salt-producers on the Cheshire Plain, and towns to the east like Nottingham and Sheffield.

Access: 5 miles south-west of Buxton (on B5053).

Crewe and Harpur Arms

Market Square. Tel (01298) 83205
Grid ref: 088649
Open: 12-2, 5.00-11; 11-11 Sat; 12- 10.30 Sun.
Beer: Marston's Bitter and either Marston's Pedigree or Bass, plus one guest beer such as Timothy Taylor's Landlord.
Food: Full menu of hot and cold food served lunchtime and evening, in either of the two bars or no-smoking dining room. 'Steak specials' on Friday evening, plus the 5-course Sunday roast is also very popular (booking advisable). Up to six main meal vegetarian options, including stilton and vegetable crumble, and tropical vegetable curry.

Accommodation: B&B - 7 en-suite rooms (doubles, singles, and family); 3 self-catering cottages, and apartment above pub; small camping and caravan site (5 stands), with toilets and showers.

General: Named after the Harpur-Crewe family, former lords of Longnor Manor. The inn was once part of the Harpur-Crewe estate of Calke Abbey, Ticknall (south of Derby), and today the handsome brick frontage and colourful flower borders makes this an eye-catching building. Apart from the tables at the front, there's outside seating at the rear with terrific views across the Manifold valley. Families welcome (small adventure playground at the back); and wheelchair ramps and disabled toilets in place.

Horseshoe Inn, Longnor

Horseshoe Inn

Longnor Tel (01298) 83262
Grid ref: 087649
Open: 11-11; 12-10.30 Sun.
Beer: Marston's Bitter, Pedigree; Cameron's Strongarm, plus two guest beers. Also look out for Weston's strong cider - at 9% ABV it is described by the landlord as "extremely nasty".
Food: Light snacks only (sandwiches, pasties, etc) served all day.
General: Built in 1609, this pleasant and welcoming pub consists of a main knocked-

West

through bar, with a newly-restored open fireplace and a pool table in a rear room. Every Friday there's live music variously featuring folk, blues, country and western, etc (free), and plans are also afoot to develop 'pub theatre'. There are a couple of pavement-edge tables outside, and the geniality of the place is summarised in the following sign that often appears by the door: 'kids, dogs, boots welcome'.

MEERBROOK - Staffordshire

This quiet hamlet is a good location from which to explore Tittesworth Reservoir, where Severn Trent has built a visitor centre, nature trail, etc; and the small but spectacular ridge known as The Roaches, a jagged line of rocks that thrust up into the sky from the empty moorland. There are plenty of footpaths, including the Staffordshire Moorlands Walk, plus rock climbing on The Roaches and fishing on the reservoir.

Access: 2 miles north of Leek (off A53).

Half the population of Britain live within 60 miles of the Peak District

Lazy Trout

Meerbrook Tel (01538) 300385
Grid ref: 990607
Open: 11.30-2.30, 6-11 (closed Tues eve in winter); 11-11 Sat; 12-10.30 Sun.
Beer: Banks's Bitter; Marston's Pedigree, and one guest beer (previously Otter King, Shepherd Neame Spitfire, etc).
Food: Appetising menu and specials board board offering the likes of Chinese stir fry, and chicken, ham & mushroom or lamb & mint pudding; plus a range of lunchtime sandwiches and snacks. Fresh trout periodically available via the fishermen on nearby Tittesworth Reservoir - if they've been lucky! Served in bar or no-smoking dining area from 11.3-2, 6-8.30, Mon-Fri, 11/12-2.30, 6-9/8.30 Sat/Sun.
General: Since it was built over 300 years ago, the original building has been added to and developed, and today it's an attractive whitewashed pub sitting opposite Meerbrook Youth Hostel. The present owners have developed the garden at the rear, which has children's swings and good

views of The Roaches. Inside, the main room is illuminated by large, low windows and a log fire in winter, while to the other side of the bar is a separate dining room. Families and walkers welcome.

NEW MILLS - Derbyshire

The Rivers Sett and Goyt once provided the power for numerous mills - originally corn, then later cotton-spinning - that earned the town its prosperity and of course its name, but although some local industry remains there is a growing emphasis on recreation. A former railway branch line has been converted to the Sett Valley Trail, a short and traffic-free route of 3 miles from New Mills to Hayfield. Meanwhile, below New Mills Central railway station in the dramatic Torrs gorge, the award-winning Millennium Walkway provides an exciting aerial walking route above the gushing River Goyt. Opposite is Torr Vale Mill, now redundant but listed by English Heritage as the longest continuously worked cotton mill in the country. There's more details about these and other local attractions in a fascinating exhibition at the new Heritage Centre (at the back of the bus station), but sadly the unremarkable pubs of New Mills won't figure too highly on most visitors' itineraries. The two exceptions are given below, although the Packhorse Inn is actually a mile out of town on the road to Mellor.

Beehive

Albion Road (A6015). Tel (01663) 742087
Grid ref: 998851
Open: 5-11 Mon-Wed; 11-11 Thurs-Sat; 12-10.30 Sun.
Beer: Boddingtons Bitter; Storm Ale Force (from Storm Brewing Company of Macclesfield), plus two guest beers.
Food: A few light snacks, served 5 till mid evening, such as chicken and lamb tikka, and kebabs.
General: Bright and stylish, this modernised corner pub to the south of the main shops (Albion Road connects with the A6) adopts an almost city bar style, with tiled floor and light wooden furniture and decor. It's run in conjunction with a smart

Indian restaurant and take-away upstairs, and so offers the unusual but happy opportunity to combine decent real ale with serious curry. Disabled toilet; families and dogs welcome; small yard with outside seating.

Packhorse Inn

Mellor Road (north of New Mills).
Tel (01663) 742365
www.packhorseinn.co.uk
Grid ref: 002870
Open: 12-3, 5-11, 11-11 Sat; 12-10.30 Sun.

Beer: Tetley Bitter, plus three guest beers from regional breweries such as Phoenix, Belvoir and Hogs Back.

Food: Full set menu featuring baked potatoes, seafood casserole, grills and steaks, plus daily specials board and curry of the week. Served 12-2, 6-10 Mon-Fri; all day weekends ('till 10pm Sat and 9pm on Sun).

Accommodation: B&B - en-suite rooms - 2 double, 2 twin, 1 double/single.

General: Very neat and attractive old pub set in the hillside a mile north of New Mills, with glorious views over the valley and town, as well as east to the wild uplands of Kinder Scout. The terraced garden to the rear, lined with colourful troughs and pots, is especially delightful. Inside it's basically one light, open room, with a wood-burning stove, but planning permission has just been given for the construction of a new dining room. Children welcome 'till 9pm; no dogs.

ONECOTE - Staffordshire

A small village on the Staffordshire Moorlands, to the west of the Manifold valley, and pronounced locally 'Onkut'.

Access: 4 miles east of Leek.

Jervis Arms

Onecote (on B5053). Tel (01538) 304206
Grid ref: 050552
Open: 12-3, 7-11; 12-3, 7-10.30 Sun.

Beer: Bass, plus four guest beers, such as Whim Hartington Bitter; Titanic Lifeboat; Abbeydale Belfry etc.

Food: Reasonably-priced menu ranges from sandwiches and light snacks to hot meals, and blackboard choices include

pork ragout, chicken fillet in stilton and pork in cider. Vegetarian and children's menu available. Served 12-2, 7-10 (6-10 Sat), and 12-9.30pm on Sun. No-smoking and family room available.

General: Although much changed since its 17th century origins, this large pub on Onecote's main road has a riverside lawn - the infant Hamps River - with picnic tables swings and slides, and a footbridge across to the car park. Inside it's modern but comfortable, with a large dining area and an elegant stone fireplace. Children are welcome in the family and no-smoking rooms, and there's an entrance ramp for wheelchair users.

RAINOW - Cheshire

The pub is located about a mile north-east of the village of Rainow, near Bollington, and is known locally as 'the patch'. Its rural, picturesque situation makes it a popular stop for walkers and cyclists.

Access: 3 miles nort-east of Macclesfield, on the B5470.

Highwayman

Whaley Bridge Road (B5470).Tel (01625) 573245
Grid ref: 963773
Open: 12-2.30 (3 Sat), 7-11; 12-3, 7-10.30 Sun.

Beer: Thwaites Bitter.

Food: Set menu includes range of hot and cold pub food, plus a selection of Mexican specialities (burritos, enchiladas, tortillas), served 12-2, 7-9.15.

General: Handsome, whitewashed 16th century building, comprising four small and atmospheric dark rooms with open fires, low-beamed ceilings and carved oak benches. Until 1949 it was known as the Blacksmiths Arms, and by all accounts is haunted - look out for the ghostly old man sitting in the corner of the snug, and the mysterious smoke rings that appear in the middle room! Families welcome, but no dogs. A few benches out the front provide good views over the open countryside towards Manchester.

> *Only 4.2% of the Peak Park is owned by the National Park Authority – the rest is in private hands*

West

STRINES - Greater Manchester

A linear settlement situated between the River Goyt and Peak Forest Canal.
Access: 1 mile south-east of Marple (on B6101).

Sportsman's Arms

105 Strines Road (B6101). Tel (0161) 427 2888
Grid ref: 969868
Open: 12-3, 5.30-11 Mon-Fri; 11-11 Sat; 12-10.30 Sun.
Beer: Cains Bitter, Dark Mild; Boddingtons Bitter, plus one guest beer.
Food: Good range of traditional pub food, including sandwiches, steak baguette, and a variety of muffins, plus main dishes and daily specials such as Thai curry, brie crumble, and mushroom stroganoff. Served 12-2, 6-9 Mon-Fri, 12-2, 6-10 Sat, and all day Sun 'till 9pm.
General: The main, lounge bar is open and spacious, with a massive main window to take advantage of wide views over the Goyt valley. Comfortable seating and an open fire also make it a cosy evening venue. Dogs in Vault (public) bar only. Families welcome. Outside seating on small side terrace.

THORNCLIFFE - Staffordshire

A hamlet on the edge of the Staffordshire Moorlands near Tittesworth Reservoir and the Roaches.
Access: Two miles north-east of Leek, off the A53.

Mermaid Inn

Thorncliffe. Tel (01538) 300253
www.themermaidinn.com
Grid ref: 036605
Open: 12-3 (closed Mon, Tue lunch) 7-11; 12-3. 7-10.30 Sun.
Beer: One changing beer (such as Greene King IPA; Marston's Pedigree; John Smiths Bitter).
Food: Bar food or à la carte menu in what is supposedly one of the highest restaurants in England (around 1,500 ft) - the views on a clear day are said to include the mountains of North Wales. Specials include rack of Derbyshire lamb, breast of Barbary duck, and filo pastry parcels of cream

cheese, spinach and sweet peppers. Served 12-2, 7-9 (not Mon or Tues lunchtime).
General: Nearby is a small, bleak moorland pool (Blake Mere, or Blakemere Pool) where according to legend a young woman was drowned as a witch, and since then has haunted the bottomless waters as a siren or mermaid. The inn is located 1 $\frac{1}{2}$ miles north-east of Thorncliffe, sitting alone on an exposed hilltop road. The views are impressive, but the wind can be raw, so you'll probably end up inside the large, rambling building, which welcomes families and dogs.

WHALEY BRIDGE - Derbyshire

A small town on the north-western edge of the Peak National Park near New Mills, located in the pretty Goyt valley. The Industrial Revolution inspired first coal-mining and then a string of textile mills to appear along the valley. Before long the Peak Forest Canal was extended to reach Whaley and although the industry has now mostly gone the small wharf remains busy with colourful narrow boats. Other leisure-seekers use the town as a base for walking the surrounding hills, as well as wanders along the Goyt valley - there are paths south to Fernilee and Errwood Reservoirs.
Access: The town is on the A5004 Whaley Bridge - Buxton road, or easy access from the A6 Buxton - Manchester route.

Goyt Inn

8 Bridge Street. Tel (01663) 732840
Grid ref: 013816
Open: 12-3, 5-11; 12-3, 5-10.30 Sun.
Beer: Worthington Bitter; Bass; Tetley Bitter.
Food: Snacks and meals served lunchtime only - from sandwiches and toasties to chilli, pies and Sunday roast; plus home-made milk shakes.
General: Tucked away on a side street opposite the station, this small but handsome one-bar pub is a dark and cosy with open fires and wooden beams. There's a couple of seats at the front and a sheltered yard at the back, although children, dogs, etc. are welcome inside. The waterways theme runs throughout the pub, and canal-goers and walkers are regular patrons.

Navigation Inn

6 Johnson Street. Tel (01663) 732308
Grid ref: 013813
Open: 11-11; 12-10.30 Sun.
Beer: Boddingtons Bitter, plus a guest beer (often from Robinson's Brewery).
Food: Standard range of pub food served daily 12-4, and in evening if booked in advance.
General: Located near the canal wharf at the northern end of town, this mid 18th century hostelry has an attractive exterior with hanging baskets and seats by the front door. Inside, plush open-plan seating surrounds a central bar, and in the front there's usually live music (a solo artist or duo) every weekend.

Shepherds Arms

7 Old Road. Tel (01663) 732384
Grid ref: 013813
Open: 11-11; 12-10.30 Sun.
Beer: Marston's Bitter, Pedigree; Banks's Bitter, plus one seasonal Martson's beer.
Food: Sandwiches and toasties every day 'till around 4 pm.
General: Pleasantly unspoilt town centre pub, sitting above the main road (A5004). It has two outdoor terraces, with plenty of seating, to the side of the solid white-washed building (supposedly the second oldest in the town). Inside, the lounge bar is old-fashioned but homely, containing a rocking chair and mementos of the Whaley Bridge Cricket Club whose base this is. The stone-flagged tap room is typically bare with no frills. Families, dogs welcome.

WHITEHOUGH - Derbyshire

Situated midway between Whaley Bridge and Chapel-en-le-Frith, this hamlet lies just south of Chinley off the B6062.

Oddfellows Arms

Whitehough Head Lane. Tel (01663) 750306
Grid ref: 039820
Open: 11-11; 12-10.30 Sun.
Beer: Marston's Bitter, Pedigree, Mild, plus two guest beers.
Food: Served all day 'till 8pm, the set menu and specials board features a range of hot and cold fare from baguettes and sand-wiches through to pies and steaks.
General: Originally the Princes Arms and located on the main road through the centre of Whitehough, this 18th century building has a cosy and looked-after feel, with real fires and small but attractive open rooms. Walkers and cyclists are welcome, as are families and dog-owners (inside and out). No piped music or jukebox; a couple of benches by the roadside at front.

WILDBOARCLOUGH - Cheshire

A remote hamlet that once supported three silk mills, it's tucked away in a narrow and secluded clough (valley), surrounded by vast swathes of rough open moorland and the arresting shape of Shutlingsloe. This 1,659 ft hill rises behind the pub like a miniature Matterhorn, and the path to the top leads off a farm track just along the lane (it's not that far in terms of distance, and the views from the top are superb).
Access: 7 miles south-west of Buxton (off A54).

Crag Inn

Wildboarclough. Tel (01260) 227239
Grid ref: 982685
Open: 12-3, 7-11; 12-3, 7-10.30 Sun.
Beer: Morland Old Speckled Hen; Timothy Taylor's Landlord; Worthington Bitter.
Food: Served 12-2 (12-3 at weekends), 7-9pm, in large, open bar, or Fri eve and Sun lunchtime carvery in no-smoking dining room. Blackboard menu includes pies, fish, half a roasted duck in cranberry and whisky sauce, and bilberry pie, plus light snacks and wholemeal rolls with a range of fillings.
Accommodation: Self-catering holiday flat available.
General: This large, 17th century farm-house became an inn in the 1830s, and comprises one spacious, high-ceilinged room with plenty of tables, open fires, and adorned with various stuffed animals. Families welcome, but no dogs inside. Popular with walkers, there's a large patio area outside, but booted walkers can go indoors using plastic bootcovers provided.

Pipe measure - 115 gallons of port

Strines – Whaley Bridge

West

WINCLE - Cheshire

An out-of-the-way hamlet situated in the lovely Dane valley, just across the river from Danebridge. The area, and hence the pub, is not surprisingly popular with walkers and discerning visitors to this sometimes overlooked corner of the National Park. **Access:** 9 miles south-west of Buxton (off A54).

Ship Inn

Wincle. Tel (01260) 227217
Grid ref: 963653
Open: 12-3, 7-11 (closed Mon); Sat 12-4, 6-11; Sun 12-4, 7-10.30.

Beer: Boddingtons Bitter; York Yorkshire Terrier, plus one guest beer often from the nearby Beartown Brewery or Storm Brewing Company.

Food: Small but quality range of choices from blackboard, including sirloin steak, locally caught trout, home-made nut roast, and aubergine mousse, plus sandwiches and baguettes (weekends) at lunchtimes. Wednesday is the popular fresh fish day. Served in either of two bars or small no-smoking dining room, Tues-Fri 12-2, 7-9 ('till 9.30pm on Fri), weekends 12-2.30, 7-9.30 ('till 9pm on Sun). Booking advisable for Wed and weekends.

General: Picturesque, 16th century inn on quiet lane, knocked through from three separate cottages. It was renamed after Shackleton's successful Antarctic expedition of 1907, since his team included Sir Philip Lee Brocklehurst of nearby Swythamley Hall (and their ship, Nimrod, is depicted in the pub sign). There are three small, simple but attractive rooms, including a hiker's bar/family room and no-smoking dining room (dogs in former only). Small beer garden by the car park to rear, and benches out front.

Barley to Beer - a short guide to brewing

The basic ingredients needed to produce beer are barley, yeast, water and hops. The process begins with the production of malted barley. The grains are soaked in water and spread over the malting floor, where they are allowed to germinate. This causes the starch in the grains to be converted to a form of sugar, which is necessary for fermentation. Germination is stopped at the appropriate time by heat treatment. At this early stage the brewer can affect the flavour and type of beer by his choice of barley and the amount of heat applied. Higher temperatures produce a roasted malt giving a darker beer, whilst a lower temperature gives a paler malt and therefore a paler beer. The malt is then crushed and mixed with water, and heated in a large container called a mash tun. This allows the sugars in the malt to dissolve in the water. As the hot mash is a mixture of liquid and solids, it must be filtered before the next stage.

Following filtration the liquid is known as wort and is transferred to a copper where it is boiled. The evaporation increases the gravity of the wort and also kills any bacteria. During the boiling stage the all-important hops are added, crucial to the flavour of the beer, they also act as a preservative and clearing agent. Different varieties of hops will give different levels of bitterness, and impart an aroma to the beer. Commonly used varieties in English beer are Fuggles, Goldings and Maris Otter. Instead of hops, some specialist beers may use other flavourings such as ginger, orange peel, fruits, or even seaweed!

After the boiling process the wort again needs filtering to separate out the used hops and any other solid material. The wort is then cooled before being transferred to the fermentation vessel. Yeast is added and the the vessel is carefully warmed to allow fermentation to begin, this converts the sugars present in the wort to alcohol. The strain of yeast used is important in determining the flavour and other characteristics of the beer. Using a yeast grown from a single strain, also helps brewers to attain consistency. (Yeast occurs naturally in the air, and some Belgian beers, known as lambic beers, undergo spontaneous fermentation using airbourne yeast). After this initial fermentation the beer is not yet ready for drinking, and is run into a tank for a maturing period where secondary fermentation continues at a slower rate. Before being racked into casks the beer may then be filtered and pasteurised to stop fermentation and give a beer with a long shelf-life. This is 'keg' beer and is normally dispensed using carbon dioxide, or nitrogen (in the case of 'smooth' beers). For real ale the beer is not filtered, but is allowed to continue fermenting and maturing in the cask. It is a 'live' product with much more flavour and aroma than the pasteurised keg beers.

Part Four: Southern Area

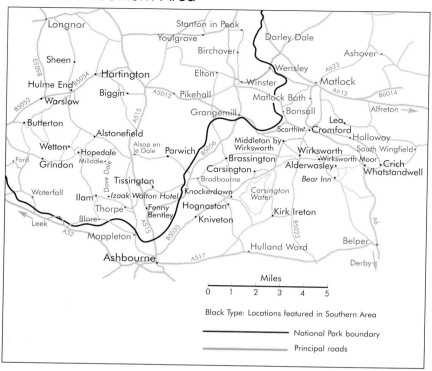

Longnor

Stanton in Peak

Darley Dale

Youlgrave

Birchover

Ashover

Sheen

Elton

Wensley

Hartington

A623

Matlock

Hulme End

Winster

B5054

B5053

Biggin

A5012

Pikehall

Matlock Bath

A615

B6014

Warslow

Bonsall

Alfreton

Grangemill

Butterton

Scarthin

Lea

Cromford

Alstonefield

Middleton by
Wirksworth

Holloway

Wetton

Alsop en
le Dale

Parwich

B5056

Wirksworth

South Wingfield

Hopedale

Brassington

Wirksworth Moor

Ford

Milldale

Alderwasley

Crich

Grindon

Carsington

Whatstandwell

Tissington

Bradbourne

Bear Inn

Waterfall

Ilam

Izaak Walton Hotel

Knockerdown

Carsington
Water

Thorpe

Fenny
Bentley

Hognaston

Leek

Blore

Kniveton

Kirk Ireton

A52

B5023

A6

Mappleton

A535

Belper

Hulland Ward

Ashbourne

A517

Derby

Miles

0 1 2 3 4 5

Black Type: Locations featured in Southern Area

━━━━━━━━━━ National Park boundary

━━━━━━━━━━ Principal roads

ALDERWASLEY - Derbyshire

Alderwasley (locally pronounced "Allers-ley") is a small and rather scattered village located midway between Wirksworth and Whatstandwell, although the Bear Inn is actually on a road that passes to the south of the village.

Access: Leave the B5035 at the crossroads at Wirksworth Moor, taking the road south. After approximately 1½ miles the pub will be seen on the left hand side of the road.

Bear Inn

Alderwasley. Tel (01629) 822585
Grid ref: 315527
Open: 11-11; 12-10.30 Sun.

Beer: Bass; Marston's Pedigree, plus two guest beers.

Food: Blackboard menu, which changes regularly, with mouth-watering dishes such as fruit curry with papaya and mango, tuna steaks, duck breast, parmesan and spring onion potato cakes, etc. Served 12-9 daily throughout the pub, with Sunday carvery in dining room. Booking advisable at popular times due to limited number of tables. Extensive wine list, plus hot mulled wine.

Accommodation: B&B - 8 en-suite double bedrooms, including one 4-poster.

General: Sitting isolated on a hilltop between Wirksworth and the Derwent valley, this large and rambling late Tudor coaching inn oozes atmosphere and charm. From the caged birds to the roaring stove, the candles to the tapestries, it's a wonderful grotto of a place, with the small and intimate rooms all individually named (Buntings, Witches Nest, Oberon's Keep, Bear Hall). No under 14s in the bar, but separate family area available. Outside there is a large spread of picnic tables, from where you can enjoy views of the Derwent valley and distant Crich Stand.

ALSTONEFIELD - Staffordshire

Once this was quite a busy meeting of packhorse routes, with regular cattle sales taking place until only a century ago. Nowadays it's a peaceful, out-of-the-way village, situated high above the Manifold and Dove valleys, and a very popular spot

with walkers. Indeed, what can beat a leisurely day's walking in the surrounding hills and dales, followed by a well-earned pint while relaxing on the picturesque village green opposite the pub?

Access: 8 miles north of Ashbourne (off B5054 near Hartington).

George, Alstonefield

George

Alstonefield. Tel (01335) 310205
Grid ref: 131556
Open: 11-3, 6-11; 11-11 Sat; 12-10.30 Sun.

Beer: Burtonwood Bitter, plus one guest beer (from breweries such as Jennings, The Wood Brewery, Elgoods etc.)

Food: Home-made meals and snacks served daily from 12-2 and 7-9.15pm, plus a weekend afternoon menu. Includes traditional pies and flans (onion, salmon, asparagus), local trout, home-boiled ham, plus good choice of puddings. Orders are taken at the kitchen door - "so you can see what's going on," according to the landlady.

Accommodation: small campsite in croft at rear.

General: Pleasant and unspoilt 16th century coaching inn overlooking the village green. Features a small, cosy bar with real fire and fascinating array of prints and photos (plus overseas banknotes pinned to the ceiling), and a large no-smoking dining room across the hallway. With picnic tables outside at front and back, plus the inviting open green, it's the perfect destination after a summer's ramble. Children in dining room only; no dogs.

> *Say, for what were hop yards meant,*
> *Or why was Burton built on Trent?*
> A.E.Houseman

ASHBOURNE - Derbyshire

The town of Ashbourne is notable on a number of counts, not least for the handsome church of St Oswald, described by George Eliot as "the finest mere parish church in the kingdom". There are a number of fine period buildings, many of which can be found on Church Street. These include almshouses and a Tudor building that was once home to Queen Elizabeth Grammar School. Opposite this is The Mansion, the early 18th century home of Dr John Taylor, who frequently entertained his close friend Dr Samuel Johnson (see Green Man Royal Hotel entry). The sloping, cobbled market place in the town centre has seen trading since the 13th century, and on nearby St John Street is a shop that has been making and selling Ashbourne's famous gingerbread for 115 years (it is said that the original recipe came from French prisoners of war who were held captive in the town during the Napoleonic Wars). Ashbourne's location near the southern end of Dovedale makes it a popular spot with visitors approaching the Peak District from the south, plus it forms the southern terminus end of the Tissington Trail (cycle hire available). For more details call Ashbourne Tourist Information Centre on 01335 343666.

Bowling Green

2 North Avenue. Tel (01335) 342511
Grid ref: 179471
Open: Varies, but usually 11.30-3(4 Sat), 5.30-11; 12-4, 5.30-10.30 Sun.
Beer: Bass; Marston's Pedigree; Worthington Bitter.
Food: Renown for its range of high quality food, fresh and home-made, and cooked to order. Advanced booking is often essential. The main speciality is fish, including grilled whole Dover sole, poached monkfish, salmon, plaice, turbot and sea bass. Served in bar or no-smoking dining room, 12-2, 6-9.
Accommodation: B&B - 1 twin, 1 double room.
General: Situated north of the market place at the top of the short but steep hill (Buxton Road), the oldest part of this small

and rather oddly-shaped pub dates back nearly 400 years old and is named after the bowling green which once stood next door. Although it's a popular eating pub, the bar areas remain traditional and comfy, decorated with masks and carvings from Africa and the Middle East which reflect the landlady's travels.

A football match like no other

Every year on Shrove Tuesday a peculiar and vaguely dangerous sporting contest takes place that has virtually no rules, any number of competitors, no defined pitch, and whose goals are three miles apart. The two teams in Ashbourne's Shrovetide football match are known as the 'Up'ards' and 'Down'ards', depending on which side of Henmore Brook (which runs through the centre of the town) you come from. The aim is to propel a ball towards each others' goal three miles away, but in practice it usually degenerates into a sweaty scrum of bodies that heave and crawl their way backwards and forwards along the brook and across fields all day long. And if as is often the case no goal has been scored when light falls the game simply ends. It's been played (if that's the right term) each Shrove Tuesday for centuries (possibly since 1400), and its origins are unknown.

Scaffold sign, Ashbourne

Green Man Royal Hotel

St John Street. Tel (01335) 345783
Grid ref: 181467
Open: 11-11; 12-10.30 Sun.
Beer: Bass; Marston's Pedigree.
Food: Choice of snacks and hot meals from set menu and daily specials board, including pies, tortilla wraps and fresh

salad platters. Served in two bars 12-2.30, 6-8.30.

Accommodation: 12 mixed B&B rooms
General: Historic town centre pub (c1750) with a rare 'scaffold' sign spanning the main road - which true to its name was once used as a gibbet! Today's establishment is formed from the joining of two pubs in 1825 (the Green Man and Black's or Blackamoor Head), hence the figurehead on the top of the sign. The main hotel bar is a dark and comfortable oak-panelled affair, once a favourite haunt of Dr Johnson who often visited Ashbourne (and whose comments on the inn are reproduced on the wall). Next door but part of the same establishment is Grogan's, an open and trendy modern bar with widescreen TV and music. There are two open courtyards with seats; families welcome; dogs allowed inside after meal times.

> *"Nay, I am for the country liquor, Derbyshire Ale, if you please; for a man should not, methinks, come up from London to drink wine in the Peak."*
> Samuel Johnson

Smiths Tavern

St John Street. Tel (01335) 342264
Grid ref: 182467
Open: 11-3, 6-11 (11-11 summer) Mon-Thurs; 11-11 Fri, Sat; 12-10.30 Sun.
Beer: Banks's Bitter; Marston's Pedigree, plus a seasonal beer from Marstons.
Food: Set menu and changing specials board, featuring a range of traditional cooking, including freshly-prepared pies, steaks, lamb, etc. Served throughout the pub (back room no-smoking) between 12-3 and 6-9/9.30.
General: Narrow-fronted cosy old pub on Ashbourne's main thoroughfare, squeezed between a row of shops and dating back to 1686. It was formerly a monastery, and the room at the back still contains some of the furnishings from that era, including the bishop's chair. The upright piano in the middle room is slightly more modern, but no less attractive (when played well). Families welcome, dogs in bar area only.

BIGGIN - Staffordshire

A quiet if unremarkable village, but a useful base for cyclists to reach the nearby Tissington Trail, and for walkers to explore the long and wild Biggin Dale. This is part of a National Nature Reserve, a dry and unpoilt valley supporting a variety of limestone-loving plants and grasses.
Access: 1 ½ miles south-east of Hartington (off A515).

Waterloo Inn

Main Street. Tel (01298) 84284
Grid ref: 153596
Open: 11-3, 6-11 (11-11 summer)
Beer: Bass, plus one guest beer such as John Smith's Magnet or Everard's Tiger.
Food: Served in bar all day 'till mid evening (up to 10pm in summer). Full range of meals and snacks, including giant Yorkshire puddings and home-made soups.
Accommodation: Caravan and camping field to rear (includes toilets, electric hook-up, etc).
General: Bright, open pub set back from the road near the church. L-shaped bar includes a real fire and tiled floor, plus a separate pool room. Popular with walkers (large outside lawn by side), as well as locals - there are seven games teams, including darts and dominoes. Families and dogs welcome. Look out for the smart bench opposite the main bar, inscribed 'MR' (Midland Railway) and previously to be found on Derby Railway Station.

Know your drink

Black and tan - half stout and half ale
Black Velvet - champagne topped with Guinness
Bloody Mary - tomato juice with vodka
Dog's nose - ale topped with gin
Mulled (eg wine) - a warm drink with spices
Pink gin - dash of Angostura bitter with gin
Pink Panther - pernod, dash grenadine, soda
Posset - hot milk curdled with ale
Shandy gaff - beer and ginger ale
Scotch mist - Scotch whisky frappé
Snakebite - cider and lager
Stone fence - whisky in a glass of cider
Stout - dark ale brewed from black malt
Whisky mac - whisky with ginger wine

BRASSINGTON - Derbyshire

A picturesque village lying at the foot of the ridge to the north of Carsington Water, and a short distance from the High Peak Trail. It was once a busy lead-mining centre, as reflected in the name and history of one of the two pubs, although most of the shafts, 'rakes', pits and mounds are long-dormant and now grassed over. Nearby are Rainster and Harborough Rocks, which are both reachable by public footpath. The curious formations of dolomitic limestone also contain caves, some of which were inhabited until well into the 1700s. The views from the top of the rocks, across Carsington Water and the south of Derbyshire, are superb!

Access: 3 miles west of Wirksworth (off B5035 Ashbourne-Wirksworth road).

Miners Arms

Brassington. Tel (01629) 540222
Grid ref: 232544
Open 12-3, 5.30-11; 11-11 Sat; 12-10.30 Sun.
Beer: Marston's Pedigree; Banks's Bitter, Banks's Original, plus an occasional seasonal beer from Banks's.
Food: Standard range of hot and cold food, with good portions, from 'lite bites' to main meals and home-made sweets. Served 12-2 Mon-Fri, 12-3 at weekends, 6-9.30 evenings.
Accommodation: B&B - 1 double, 1 twin, 1 single.
General: When this 250-year-old village centre pub once hosted the Barmote Court, local miners had individual accounts with the landlord who gave often long credit for his fees for 'measuring the ore', as well as allowing goods and services in lieu of financial debts. It seems that together with some farming and his mining revenue, the innkeeper made a very comfortable living! Today the long, knocked-through building entertains plenty of walkers and cyclists, and also welcomes families and dogs. There are a few seats out the front, and a patio area to the rear.

Lead mining around Brassington

There are hundreds of old mines in the Brassington and Carsington area, nearly all of them very small, but with narrow shafts sometimes 300-400 feet deep that gave rise to tunnels and galleries that traced the veins of lead. The mines were prospected by local men who gave them hopeful-sounding names like Waynes Dream or Childrens Fortune, or exotic variations such as Potosi Mine (from the famous silver mine in Bolivia) and Golconda, after the rich diamond city in India. Some yielded decent supplies of lead, but many provided poor returns, and most of the miners also farmed in order to make some sort of living. The Miners Arms in the centre of the village hosted the Barmote Court, and the Barmaster (for a long time the pub landlord) adjudicated over contentious mining claims, as well as giving credit to miners. If a miner left a mine unworked, for reasons other than problems with ventilation or flooding, the Barmaster 'nicked' the wooden winding gear (the 'stow') at the top of his shaft once a week with his knife, and if after three weeks nothing had changed the mine could then be 'freed' by another miner (hence the origin of the term 'nicked'). For further details see 'Paupers Venture Childrens Fortune' by Ron Slack, Scarthin Books, 1986.

Olde Gate Inne

Well Street. Tel (01629) 540448
Grid ref: 231543
Open 12-2.30 (3 Sat), 6-11; 12-3, 6-10.30 Sun.
Beer: Marston's Pedigree, plus up to two beers from Banks's (such as Banks's Bitter and Old Fangled).
Food: Changing lunchtime and evening menus, from filled baguettes and omelettes to 'The Derbyshire Fidget' (baked layers of cheese, ham, potato and onion) and the 'Grimsby Crumble', plus lamb steaks, baby sole, etc. No food on Mon. Evening servings 7-8.45 Tues-Thurs, 7-9 Fri-Sat, 7-8.30 Sun. One room no-smoking.
General: Dating from 1616 and suppos-

edly incorporating timber from ships sunk at the time of the Armada, this peaceful and entirely unspoilt inn (on the Bradbourne road out of the village) oozes history and atmosphere. At the far end of the stone-flagged bar, flanked by scrubbed wooden tables, is a superb open kitchen range, while overhead are various pewters and pots. The oak-panelled lower room (with grand open fire) was once used as a temporary hospital during the Civil War, and not surprisingly there are regular reports of ghostly sightings in the building. Walkers and dogs are welcome inside, but children under 10 are only permitted in the beer garden to the rear.

> *Yorkshire Square - a fermentation vessel*

BUTTERTON - Staffordshire

A quiet and attractive, out-of-the-way sort of village lying high to the west of the Manifold valley. Hoo Brook, which feeds into the Manifold, runs below the village, and there's plenty of scenic footpaths connecting with neighbouring Warslow, Grindon and Ford.

Access: 3½ miles south-west of Hartington (off B5053).

Black Lion Inn

Butterton. Tel (01538) 304232
www.blacklioninn.co.uk
Grid ref: 076566
Open: 12-2 (closed Mon lunch), 7-11 (11-11 summer); 12-2, 7-10.30 (12-10.30 summer) Sun.
Beer: Whim Hartington Bitter; Theakston's Best Bitter; Marston's Pedigree, plus up to two guest beers.
Food: Well-priced menu of traditional hot and cold food, including sandwiches and snacks, served 12-2, 7-9.30 (not Mon lunchtime). Pub includes dining room and no-smoking area.
Accommodation: B&B - 3 double rooms, all en-suite, plus a family room.
General: Dating from 1782, this lovely village inn near the church features two bars and a series of small and intimate rooms with open fires and a superb old kitchen range. Richly decorated with plates, prints, photos and brass, there's a separate pool

room and dining room, an upright piano and plenty of tucked-away seating. Families, walkers and dogs all welcome. Outside are benches and a sheltered, terraced beer garden.

CARSINGTON - Derbyshire

This small village sits above the northern end of Carsington Water, a huge artificial reservoir (the ninth largest in England) built in the 1980s and supplying drinking water throughout the East Midlands. The visitor centre is situated on the western shore, off the B5035, and apart from the watersports and fishing there's a scenic (and quite easy) circular walking/cycling route of 7-8 miles around the entire shore. Along the way the route passes sculptures, bird hides and a woodland conservation area. Apart from a short burst of road-walking at the northern end, through the villages of Hopton and Carsington, it's quite a pleasant stroll.

Access: 2 miles west of Wirksworth (off B5035).

Miner's Arms

Main Road. Tel (01629) 540207
Grid ref: 253534
Open 12-3, 7-11 (11-11 summer); 12-3, 7-10.30 (12-10.30 summer) Sun.
Beer: Leatherbritches Miner's Slaker and Goldings; Marston's Pedigree or Bass, plus one guest beer, such as Black Sheep Best Bitter.
Food: Meals served lunchtime and evening until 9pm, bar snacks available throughout the day in summer, either in bar or no-smoking restaurant. Large portions of good quality home-made food, including proper home-made pies and specials such as salmon thermidor, banquet of lamb, plus vegetarian options. Booking advisable for popular Sunday roast.
General: A leadminers' haunt from the 1730s, it is the only pub actually on the popular circular trail around Carsington Water, and is the perfect refuelling stop for tired limbs or thirsty throats. Inside there's one long, main bar, with a parallel dining room, while outside the beer garden includes a childrens' mini adven-

South

ture playground. Specially widened doors, ramps and a disabled toilet allows wheelchair access; and there's live music every Saturday evening (varies weekly, from folk to 60s). No dogs inside.

CRICH - Derbyshire

Situated on the far south-eastern edge of the Peak District, this lofty village ('Crich' comes from the Roman for hill) is rooted in quarrying and mining, although nowadays it's best known for the award winning tramway museum. Here you can ride on lovingly restored trams from around the world along a short section of track and back, and explore the sheds and period buildings - it's a far cry from the 'Supertrams' of Sheffield and Manchester! Above the openair museum is Crich Stand, built in 1788, rebuilt in 1851 and struck by lightning in the 1890s. The present structure was built in 1923 as a memorial to the 11,409 men of the Sherwood Foresters Regiment who died in the First World War.

Access: 5 miles south-east of Matlock (on B5035).

Black Swan

Bowns Hill. Tel (01773) 852042
Grid ref: 351544
Open: 11-11; 12-10.30 Sun.
Best: Kimberley Best Bitter.
Food: Range of hot and cold meals and snacks, served 12-3, 5.30-7.30, in bars or no-smoking dining area. Includes Ramblers Special (soup and sandwich) and Dinner jackets (baked potatoes with cheese, tuna, beans, etc).
Accommodation: B&B - 2 doubles, 1 single.
General: The pub is near the centre of the village and has a high-ceilinged, wooden-panelled main bar, leading into a smaller back room with open fire, plus a separate dining area. Supposedly haunted, the building dates from the 17th century, and many years ago stood next door to the long-gone White Swan hostelry. Look out for the collection of jugs hanging from the ceiling, and the gallery of 'Peak Practice' photos in the back room. Children welcome 'till 9.30pm Fri-Sun; dogs allowed inside. Small back yard with seating.

Cliff Inn

Town End (Cromford Road). Tel (01773) 852444
Grid ref: 344548
Open: 11.30-3, 6-11; 11-11 Sat; 12-10.30 Sun.
Beer: Kimberley Best Bitter, Mild.
Food: Small but appetising choice of hot and cold meals, including sandwiches and prepared to order on local granary bread.
General: Situated just below the National Tramway Museum, to the north-west of the village, this pleasantly unpretentious pub is believed to have been originally built for the manager of the local quarry, and became a public house 100 years ago. The two small bars are simply decorated and cosy in the evenings, and there's a small courtyard plus seats by the car park at the side. Children in one bar only; dogs permitted inside.

Jovial Dutchman

Cromford Road. Tel (01773) 852421
Grid ref: 350545
Open: 12-3, 7-11; 12-3, 7-10.30 Sun.
Beers: Kimberley Best Bitter, Mild, plus seasonal Kimberley beers.
Food: Various hot and cold meals and snacks (including home-made pies, etc), served lunchtime and evenings ('till 9pm) in either bar, one of which is no-smoking.
General: Overlooking the old market cross that stands prominently in the middle of the road, this attractive building was sympathetically rebuilt in 1904, but before that it was once thatched. The unusual name is believed to date back to the heyday of the Cromford Canal (worked on by Dutch navvies), and Stephenson's light railway which once connected it to the quarry at the top of the hill. Garden at back of pub; dogs very welcome inside and out; children allowed inside if eating.

CROMFORD - Derbyshire

Cromford's claim to fame is embodied in one rather formidable but nevertheless very important man: Sir Richard Arkwright. His water-powered cotton spinning mill, built at Cromford in 1771, was the world's first, and its new techniques of mass production paved the way for the modern industrial age. Arkwright built the village to house his workforce, and despite the thundering quarry trucks, the parade above the pond is still attractive. The well-known and popular Scarthin Bookshop is located here. Cromford Mill, which is located across the A6, is slowly being renovated by the Arkwright Society, and there are displays and tours throughout the year.

Access: 2 miles south of Matlock (on A6).

Bell Inn

47 The Hill. Tel (01629) 822102
Grid ref: 294568
Open: 12-5, 7-11; 11-11 Sat; 12-10.30 Sun.
Beer: Kimberley Best Bitter, Mild, plus a Kimberley seasonal beer (such as Peddler's Pride).
General: Once called the Blue Bell, this wonderfully unspoilt local half way up the steep hill to Wirksworth was built in the mid 18th century as part of Arkwright's mill development (the building itself is listed). There are three bars, including a terrific snug, and this busy locals' pub boasts three darts teams, two football and two cricket sides. Walkers welcome, but food is not served due to the absence of a kitchen!

Boat Inn

Off Market Place, Scarthin. Tel (01629) 823282
Grid ref: 295569
Open 12-3, 6-11; 11-11 Sat; 12-10.30 Sun.
Beer: Marston's Pedigree; Mansfield Bitter, plus two guest beers (such as Fuller's London Pride; Whim Hartington Bitter).
Food: Snacks and light meals at lunchtime only.
General: Recently acquired by brother and sister team Kevin and Debbie White, the Boat Inn dates from 1772 when Arkwright deliberately positioned it out of sight of the Greyhound Hotel. That more imposing building was designed for the mill bosses and visiting businessmen, and the Boat Inn for the workers! The pub has two main bars, open fire, plus a beer cellar where it is hoped functions will take place (including Cromford's inaugural beer festival). Small sheltered beer garden at rear.

Barley Hood: old fashioned term for drunkenness or bad temper brought on by drinking

FENNY BENTLEY - Derbyshire

Despite the main road ploughing through its middle, this small village has two very interesting and certainly very different public houses. Near the Coach and Horses is Cherry Orchard Farm, which incorporates the last surviving part of Bentley Old Hall, a fortified manor house that once belonged to the Beresford family. Thomas Beresford and eight of his sons distinguished themselves at the Battle of Agincourt, and he and his wife Agnes are commemorated in an Elizabethan alabaster monument in the church of St Edmund.

Access: Two miles north of Ashbourne on the A515.

David Allingham, Landlord, Bentley Brook Inn

Bentley Brook Inn

Fenny Bentley. Tel (01335) 350278
www.bentleybrookinn.co.uk
Grid ref: 177497
Open: 11-11; 12-10.30 Sun.
Beer: Home-brewed Leatherbritches beers variously available include: Bespoke, Hairy Helmet, Ashbourne, Goldings, Belter; plus Marston's Pedigree and Mansfield Riding Bitter.
Food: Bar food available 12-9.30 (including the Sunday carvery 12-3), featuring steak & Leatherbritches ale pie, farmhouse breakfast bake, giant Yorkshire puddings, etc; and an à la carte menu is served in the no-smoking Fenny's Restaurant 12-3, 7-9.30. Typical dishes are stuffed pheasant breast, rack of lamb, and vegetarian roulade. Booking advisable at peak times when the pub can get busy.
Accommodation: B&B - 10 mixed rooms
General: This large and popular inn is sit-

South

uated on the A515 just to the south of the village centre. The imposing, half-timbered building has been much renovated over the years, and sits amid 8 acres of grounds that include a trout stream (with fishing rights), a large area of garden and ter-raced seating with barbecue, plus two outdoor skittles alleys to the rear. The high-ceilinged main room includes a central log fire, and the dining room at the far side is equally spacious and elegant. Most notably the inn is the home of Leather-britches Brewery which is located in out-buildings to the rear, but non-beer drinkers can also enjoy a range of wines and ground coffees.

Leatherbritches Brewery

The brewery was established on the site of the Bentley Brook Inn in 1995, since when it has gone from strength to strength and supplies not only shops and retail outlets but also pubs through-out the area. Its curious name harks back to the Middle Ages, when officials known as ale conners would go around checking the strength and suitability of new brews. Other than tasting it, a com-mon method was to pour a little of the beer on a bench and sit in it for 30 min-utes - if the ale conner's breeches were semi-stuck to the bench then the brew was of a satisfactory strength! Not sur-prisingly an ale conner's outfit came to include a pair of leather breeches. The Leatherbritches brewery produces half a dozen primary beers, from strong ones such as Bespoke (5% ABV) to the popular Hairy Helmet. There are some specialist brews, including a porter, and others are produced for special occasions. The whole production - from brewing to bot-tling - takes place in small outbuildings to the rear of the pub, and when the wort and hops are boiling you can often catch the wonderful aroma drifting across the car park. Viewing and visits are available by prior arrangement. Selected bottled beers are for sale over the bar. This enterprising brewery has plans to market the bottled beers through selected supermarkets.

Coach and Horses

Fenny Bentley. Tel (01335) 350246
Grid ref: 176499
Open: 11-3, 5-11; 11-11 Sat; 12-10.30 Sun.
Beer: Marston's Pedigree, plus one guest beer such as Whim Hartington Bitter or beers from Bateman's, Charles Wells etc.
Food: Appetising blackboard menu which changes regularly, and features dishes such as Tissington pork and apricot sausages, roasted vegetable pancake topped with melted brie, and steak and stilton pie. Trad-itional roast on Sundays, plus children's menu, sandwiches, etc. also available. Ser-ved throughout the pub 12-2.30 (Mon-Fri) and 12-9 at weekends. Two areas are no-smoking.
General: During its days as a coaching inn this attractive, 400-year-old establish-ment would have seen plenty of action, since it sits at the foot of a long uphill stretch. Mind you, today's car-bound visi-tors on the A515 still have plenty of reason to visit what is a cosy and welcoming family-run pub. The one main bar leads to a pleasantly tucked-away back area, plus a separate dining room. There are open fires, a flagged floor, and attractive pine benches made by the landlord's father. Families welcome; some outside seating in summer.

GRINDON- Staffordshire

A peaceful little village high on the wes-tern rim of the Manifold valley.
Access: 2½ miles north of Waterhouses, off A523/B5053.

Cavalier

Grindon. Tel (01538) 304285
Grid ref: 086543
Open: 7-11 Fri (closed Mon-Thurs - may open by prior arrangement with groups); 12-2.30, 7-11 Sat; 12-2.30, 7-10.30 Sun & Bank Holidays .
Beer: Theakston's Best Bitter; Courage Directors.
Food: Served lunchtime only, the short but appetising menu includes sandwiches and light snacks such as home-made soups - typically ham, turkey and chestnut, leek and thyme, lightly-spiced carrot, all accompan-ied by freshly-baked bread.

General: Originally the village smithy, and previously called the Shoulder of Mutton, this 400 year old building was possibly renamed in honour of Bonnie Prince Charlie, who once stayed in the village. Today it's a popular destination for walkers, and with advanced notice the pub will open specially for groups. Otherwise, time your visit carefully in order to enjoy the handsome and tastefully-decorated interior, with its open fire and tiled floor, as well as the mounted displays of old swords and armour. Small beer garden at front. Families welcome. Dogs allowed inside.

> *For details of public transport in the Peak District call Staffordshire Busline on 01785 223344 (0815-1730, M-F, 0830-1330, Sat)*

HARTINGTON - Derbyshire

This large limestone village is pleasant and full of interest, but can become very busy in the summer and on Sundays, when parking can be a problem. The village is an interesting mix of architectural styles - just up a hill to the south of the centre, is the elegant 17th century Hartington Hall (now a popular youth hostel). There is a cheese shop by the duckpond which sells the famous blue-veined stilton made in the nearby cheese factory. The village also has its own brewery (see adjacent box) and of course is located amidst some of the finest walking scenery in the White Peak, the most well-known of all being nearby Dovedale. The two pubs, both former coaching inns, are to be found opposite each other on the open main square.

Access: 7 miles south-west of Ashbourne on B5054 (off A515).

Charles Cotton Hotel

Market Place. Tel (01298) 84229
www.charlescotton.co.uk
Grid ref: 127604
Open: 11-11; 12-10.30 Sun.
Beer: Marston's Pedigree; Charles Wells Bombardier; Whim Hartington Bitter, plus usually one guest beer.
Food: Served all day from noon 'till mid or even late evening depending on demand, in bar or no-smoking dining area. Meals include steak pudding, a range of home-

-made soups, and Staffordshire oatcakes with various fillings (such as asparagus and ham, mushroom and black pudding, broccoli and brie with white onion sauce).
Accommodation: B&B - 17 mixed rooms.
General: Large, rather sombre-looking hotel off the main square, with the dark and enclosed bar at the back and spacious dining room to the front. It used to be called the Sleigh Arms, after a local family, but changed its name to cash in on the fame of one of the co-authors of 'The Compleat Angler.' Outside tables at front and rear; families welcome; dogs allowed inside.

Whim Brewery, Hartington
Located amid empty, rolling fields a couple of miles down a narrow lane south of the village of Hartington, the tiny Whim Brewery is one of the last remaining in the Peak District. It's been going since 1993 and produces a number of quality beers. The four regularly brewed beers are Hartington Bitter, Hartington IPA, Arbor Light and Magic Mushroom. The beers all have a distinctive character and flavour - Arbor Light is a pale golden, refreshing beer with a subtle hop flavour, whilst Magic Mushroom is a mild, with a stronger burnt malt flavour. The brewery also produces several seasonal beers such as Old Izaak, a dark and stronger winter brew. Whim Brewery supplies a number of pubs throughout Derbyshire and Staffordshire, and has its own tied house - The Wilkes Head in Leek.

Devonshire Arms

Hartington. Tel (01298) 84232
Grid ref: 128604
Open 11.30-3, 6-11 (11-11 summer); 12-3, 7-11 (12-10.30 summer) Sun.
Beer: Bass; Burton; Tetley's Bitter.
Food: Set menu includes light snacks and full meals, such as Drunken Bull (sirloin steak in Guinness) and the Devonshire Arms casserole, while the daily specials range from guinea fowl to red snapper. Served in either of two small bars, or the large and newly-refurbished dining room next door.

South

Accommodation: B&B - 2 doubles, 2 twin, 2 single.

General: Believed to date back as far as the 1500s and once owned by the Duke of Devonshire, the main part of the pub comprises two small and cosy bars, with low ceilings and an open fire in winter. The more modern section is to the left and incorporates the large and comfortable new dining room. Look out for the blocked-up archway that still bears scratches and marks from their wheels of passing carriages. Booted walkers and dogs are allowed in the tap room, or the beer garden at rear. Families welcome throughout; disabled toilet planned.

HOGNASTON - Derbyshire

A small and peaceful village overlooking the western shore of Carsington Water. The church has a Norman porch with an array of carved symbols and figures, as well as a belfry with gargoyles that date from the 15th century.

Access: 4 miles north-east of Ashbourne (off B5035).

Holly, of the Red Lion, Hognaston

Red Lion

Main Street. Tel (01335) 370396
www.lionrouge.com
Grid ref: 234507
Open 12-3, 6-11 (closed Mon); 12-10.30 Sun.
Beer: Marston's Pedigree; Bass; Morland Old Speckled Hen, plus one guest beer - often 'Holly's Best' from Leatherbritches Brewery (named after the pub's 22 year old Jack Russell).
Food: Superior range of imaginative and quality dishes from changing blackboard:

duo of lamb shanks, fruit kebabs, wild boar sausages cooked in orange and basil gravy, deep fried goat's cheese in a polenta crumb, and so on. Separate lunchtime/bar menu. Served 12-2 (2.30 at weekends) in bar or conservatory, 6.30-9 evenings. No chips; no children's menu; no-smoking area.

Accommodation: B&B - 3 en-suite double rooms.

General: Refurbished 17th century building, stylish and comfortable in an open-plan style, with real fires and a scattering of old tables that are often candlelit in the evening. Emphasis on eating (booking advisable in peak periods). Children welcome if dining (no under 7s); dogs allowed inside. Some outside seating at front.

> *"Drunk is feeling sophisticated when you can't say it."* Anon

HOPEDALE - Staffordshire

A peaceful hamlet tucked away in a valley near the village of Alstonefield.

Access: 3 ½ miles south of Hartington.

Watts Russell Inn

Hopedale. Tel (01335) 310271
Grid ref: 124549
Open: 11-11; 12-10.30 Sun.
Beer: Black Sheep Best Bitter, plus two guest beers (usually the likes of Timothy Taylor's Landlord; Marston's Pedigree, etc).
Food: Set menu and specials board served throughout pub (one side no-smoking) 12-9pm daily. From sandwiches and cold snacks to hot dishes such as chicken breast in stilton and leek sauce, and lamb in red wine and plum sauce; plus local, farm-made ice cream (including flavours like wild raspberry, Christmas Pudding, mint and pistachio).
General: This small and attractive old building, over 250 years old, is named after the wealthy magnate Jesse Watts Russell who lived at nearby Ilam Hall (see Ilam entry for more details). It's a neat and attractive place, with delightful outside seating terraces built into the steep hillside, and its proximity to Milldale and Dovedale makes it a popular stop for walkers. The

comfortable interior revolves around one central bar, whose decoration incorporates historic old barrels found in the cellar during refurbishment. No dogs inside; no children under 5.

HULME END - Staffordshire

A hamlet by the ancient crossing of the River Manifold, once a ford and now a handsome stone bridge, 1 1/2 miles west of Hartington (B5054). The former station building of the Leek & Manifold Light Railway (see box) is now home to the Manifold Valley Visitor Centre.

Leek & Manifold Valley Light Railway

Between 1904-34 Hulme End was the northern terminus for a curious narrow gauge line called the Leek & Manifold Valley Light Railway. The 9-mile valley bottom route followed the twists and turns of the Rivers Manifold and Hamps through the dramatic limestone scenery below Wetton Hill and Thor's Cave, and ended at Waterhouses where it joined the main line. It was built to supply remote hamlets and farmsteads with coal and other provisions, and also to bring out milk and cheese from the dairy at Ecton. The four little yellow carriages - plus milk van and two trucks - were hauled by very handsome miniature steam engines, and because they had originally been built to an Indian design they incorporated massive headlamps and equipment to attach 'cow catchers' (neither were ever used!). The railway was rather unkindly called 'a line starting nowhere and ending up at the same place', and today it's now a tarmac trail known as the Manifold Way which can be followed on foot or by bicycle.

Manifold Inn

Hulme End. Tel (01298) 84537
Grid ref: 106594
Open 12-2.30/3, 7-11; 12-2.30/3, 7-10.30 Sun.
Beer: Marston's Pedigree; Mansfield Bitter; Whim Hartington Bitter.
Food: Set choices of hot and cold food, snacks and main meals, with tasty-sounding specials such as duck breast in orange sauce, lamb mint casserole, and 'toffee lumpy bumpy' for dessert. Served 12-2, 7-9pm daily in either bar or mainly no-smoking dining room.
Accommodation: B&B - 4 en-suite doubles and 1 twin room.
General: A small but solid, 200 year-old coaching inn that stands opposite the toll-house by the old bridge over the River Manifold. It has had something of an identity crisis over the years, variously being called the Jolly Carter, Wagon and Horses and Manifold Valley Hotel, until its present renaming a few years ago. Inside it's comfortable and quite plush, with an open fire in the main area, and an unusual high seat built at the end of the bar. Walkers and cyclists are welcome, as are children if eating (in dining area only; not after 9pm). No dogs, but small garden at rear and picnic benches by car park at front.

> *"Was you ever in Dovedale? I assure you there are things in Debyshire as noble as in Switzerland and Greece."* Lord Byron

ILAM - Staffordshire

This small estate village was redesigned by the 19th century industrialist Jesse Watts Russell, who was also responsible for the mock-Gothic style of Ilam church and Hall. It is said that the angular peaks of Dove Dale reminded him of the Alps, hence the distinctive Alpine appearance of some of the buildings! Ilam Hall was partly demolished in the 1930s, and what remains now houses a youth hostel and National Trust tearoom and visitor centre. The Izaak Walton Hotel, just to the east of the village below Bunster Hill, is a short walk from the famous stepping stones at the foot of Dove Dale.
Access: 3 1/2 miles north-west of Ashbourne.

Izaak Walton Hotel

Dovedale. Tel (01335) 350555
www.izaakwalton-hotel.com
Grid ref: 144508
Open: 11-3, 6-11; 12-3, 6-10.30 Sun.
Beers: Two changing cask conditioned beers, which may include selections from the nearby Leatherbritches Brewery.

South

Food: Set menu and specials board, including trout tamara, oatcake Antionette and chicken Verona, plus light snacks and baguettes (turkey and cranberry, smoked salmon and cream cheese). Served 12-2 and 6-9 in bar or no-smoking restaurant.
Accommodation: 30 en-suite bedrooms.
General: This well-sited hotel welcomes walkers and day guests to its elegant and comfortable Dovedale Bar and Restaurant. The bar feautures some fine pieces of beautifully carved oak furniture. There are separate disabled toilets. Families and dog owners are welcome. The spacious lawn garden is the summer attraction, with its dramatic views towards Dovedale.

KIRK IRETON- Derbyshire

Quiet village in the low hills 3 miles south of Wirksworth (off B5023).

Barley Mow

Kirk Ireton. Tel (01335) 370306
Grid ref: 266502
Open 12-2, 7-11; 12-2, 7-10.30 Sun.
Beer: Served by gravity from up to six barrels, which usually include Hook Norton Old Hooky; Marston's Pedigree; Whim Hartington IPA.
Food: Filled rolls served lunchtime only.
Accommodation: B&B - 5 en-suite rooms.
General: Elegant and utterly unspoilt two-storey gabled building dating from the 17th century. It comprises three simply furnished rooms, with either tiled or wooden parquet floors, open fires or stoves, and look out for the slate tables in the bar made from a former billiards table. No fruit machines or piped music - this is a place for conversation over a decent pint. Children in back room only; dogs in bar; outside seating.

KNIVETON - Derbyshire

This small village, which apparently means 'Cengifu's farm', is located on the B5035 two miles north-east of Ashbourne. Cengifu's identity might have been lost to time, but records show that the Old Hall to the south of the village centre was for a long time the family seat of the Kniveton family until Sir Andrew's ill-fated allegiance to Charles I.

Angela Pegram, Landlady, Red Lion, Kniveton

Red Lion

Kniveton (on B5035). Tel (01335) 345554
Grid ref: 207503
Open 12-2, 7-11; 12-2, 7-10.30 Sun.
Beer: Black Sheep Best Bitter or Burton Bridge Bitter, plus one guest beer.
Food: Usual range of hot and cold food, from sandwiches to main meals, served 12-2 and 7-9 (far end of bar no smoking). But make sure to look out for imaginative range of vegetarian dishes, such as chickpea curry, baked marrow, butterbean and cider casserole, spinach and chopped nut pastie.
General: Welcoming and unassuming village local on the main road, there has been a pub here for about 300 years. Three cottages have been knocked through to create the pub as it is today. Comfortable and cosy (open fire) but not over-decorated, darts and dominoes are both popular, and in summer there's outdoors skittles. Children are welcome lunchtimes and early evenings; tables out front in summer.

KNOCKERDOWN - Derbyshire

Situated on the B5035 (Ashbourne-Wirksworth road) near the turning for Carsington Water.

Knockerdown Inn

Near Carsington Water. Tel (01629) 540209
Grid ref: 234519
Open: 11-30-2.30, 6-11 (11-11 summer);
11-30-2.30, 6-10.30 (12-10.30 summer) Sun.
Beer: Marston's Pedigree.
Food: Set menu and changing specials board, from light snacks to pies, puddings and steaks, plus Sunday lunch and 'Hillbilly

Young Diner's Menu'. Served 11.30-2.30, 6-8.30 (9.30 at weekends); no-smoking in one area of bar, plus dining room.

Accommodation: Camping and caravan site in adjoining field (with toilets), open Easter-Sept.

General: The original 17th century farm became a pub in the 1830s, and used to be called the Greyhound. Today it's a very popular family dining pub, especially in summer, partly due to its proximity to Carsington Water. The pub's children-friendly grounds include patio seating next to a large adventure playground, plus a farmyard area with donkeys, chickens and ostriches. Wheelchair access and disabled toilets. Dogs allowed inside.

"The five stages of drinking: verbose, jocose, lachrymose, bellicose, comatose." Anon.

LEA - Derbyshire

The straggling hilltop villages of Lea and neighbouring Holloway are perhaps best known for their connections with Florence Nightingale (see separate text). Also worth a visit are Lea Gardens, which every spring and early summer bursts into a spectacular riot of colourful azaleas, rhododendrons and alpines (open to the public daily from mid March to early July).

Access: 2 miles south-east of Matlock.

Jug and Glass

Lea Main Road. Tel (01629) 534232
Grid ref: 326576
Open 12-3, 7-11; 12-3, 7-10.30 Sun.

Beer: Mansfield Bitter; Marston's Pedigree, plus one guest beer (such as Whim Hartington Bitter).

Food: Served from 12-2 (cobs till 2.30), 7-9/9.30 and Sundays till 8, in bar areas or no-smoking restaurant. The menu is small but appetising, with a separate specials board, and highlights include Scottish beef dishes and steaks, Cod Portuguese, and a popular weekend carvery.

General: Before it was converted into a pub the Jug & Glass was part of a row of weavers' cottages built by Florence Nightingale's uncle in the early 1780s. Today the dark and cosy village local comprises of several small wood-panelled rooms (one

no-smoking) with comfortable seating arranged around open stoves. Picnic tables outside to front. Families welcome; live folk music every Sunday. Dogs in bar area only.

The Lady with the lamp

Although she was named after the Italian city she was born in, Florence Nightingale actually spent much of her formative early years in rural Derbyshire. The family's winter home was at Embley Park in Hampshire, but after Lea Hurst was built in the 1820s (below the village of Holloway - and now a private nursing home) they used it as their regular summer residence, and it was here that the young Florence spent much of her time educating herself in nursing and social welfare. She established local reading rooms, and helped re-house the village school in 1859, donating books and other gifts. Despite plenty of discouragement (at the time nursing was considered beneath her social position) Florence's determination was such that she took 38 nurses to Scutari and amid the horrors of the Crimea War established the first modern, military hospital. But she disliked the fuss and publicity that ensued, and although she carried on campaigning she did her best to merge back into the quiet Derbyshire countryside that she loved so much.

MIDDLETON-BY-WIRKSWORTH - Derbyshire

This village is not to be confused with Middleton by Youlgrave (Central/East area) or Stoney Middleton (North). It sits high above Wirksworth and Cromford in the middle of a busy mining area - indeed, the National Stone Centre is located in a disused quarry nearby. Passing above all this on a raised embankment is another local attraction, the High Peak Trail, a former railway line that is now a popular cycling and walking route. For those who want to explore it on two wheels, the former engine house at Middleton Top is now a visitor centre with exhibitions but also offers a cycle hire service.

Access: 1 mile north-west of Wirksworth (B5023).

South

Rising Sun

Rise End. Tel (01629) 822420
Grid ref: 279553
Open: 11-11; 12-10.30 Sun.

Beer: Marston's Pedigree; Tetley Bitter, plus occasional guest beers.

Food: Hot and cold food served 12-2.30 and 6-8.30 throughout bar or dining area (no-smoking areas by request). Set menu includes chicken rigatoni, brie crumble, and ocean pie. There are vegetarian and children's choices, plus Sunday roast.

Accommodation: B&B en-suite rooms - 2 double, 1 single.

General: A former farmhouse, this long, narrow old pub above the crossroads of the B5035/B5023 is a friendly and cosy place, with open fires at either end and comfortable leather-bound seats. Cyclists using the nearby High Peak Trail are particularly welcome, and secure overnight lock-up (the pub's cellar!) is available for bicycles, whether their owners stay at the pub or private campsite across the road - a 'Campers Breakfast' is also conveniently available for the latter (please book the night before).

PARWICH - Derbyshire

This quiet, medium-sized village (pronounced 'parr-wich') is in the low limestone hills north-west of Carsington Water. It is overlooked by Parwich Hill, on the lower slopes of which is Parwich Hall. Dating from the 1740s, it's brick and stone construction makes it quite unusual for the Peak District. The Hall was built on the site of an earlier house, just as St Peter's Church in the village centre was built from scratch in 1873 on the site of the original Norman structure.

Access: 5 miles north of Ashbourne (off A515 or B5056).

Sycamore Inn

Parwich. Tel (01335) 390212
Grid ref: 187543
Open: 12-2 (3.30 Sat), 7-11; 12-3, 7-10.30 Sun.

Beer: Robinsons Best Bitter plus one seasonal Robinsons beer, (often Old Tom).

Food: Traditional range of hot and cold bar meals, including sandwiches and light snacks, served 12-1.45 and 7-8.30 in bar

or no-smoking dining room.

General: A pleasant and unspoilt village local, dating from the late 1700s, and situated by Bradbourne Brook, near the church The sedate and handsome main bar is dominated by a huge open fireplace, and at the back is a games room (including a pool table) with an airy and simply furnished dining room across the corridor. Popular with walkers. Children in games room only. Plenty of outside seating in walled garden at front and picnic tables on lawn to side, or across the road on open grass by children's playground.

SHEEN - Staffordshire

A small village, sitting astride the narrow ridge separating the Dove and Manifold valleys, which is thought to derive its name from the old Norse word 'skjaa' (meaning shed or shelter). The pub takes its own name from the county emblem, which originated around 1400 with the Earls of Stafford. However, another rather less reliable tale suggests that a former Sheriff of Stafford devised the triple knott as a means of hanging three men at once!

Access: one mile north-west of Hartinton (off B5054)

Staffordshire Knott

Sheen. Tel (01298) 84329
Grid ref: 112612
Open: 12-2, 7-11; 12-2, 7-10.30 Sun.

Beer: Marston's Pedigree, plus one guest beer in the summer.

Food: Bar menu and baguettes served 12-2 (12-2.30 Sun), plus main meal blackboard choices also available 7-9. Changing, high quality menu includes fillet steak filled with haggis set on a quenelle of neaps and tatties finished with a Madeira sauce, and rabbit cooked in port with green figs and mushrooms. Decent wine list.

General: Attractive 17th century pub on the main street south of the village centre. The three, tastefully-decorated open rooms include a pleasant mix of old wooden chairs and carved tables, a flagged floor, and large handsome fireplace. Candle-lit in the evening, it's refined and classy. No dogs inside, but tables at the front.

Access: 9 ¹/₂ miles north-west of Ashbourne (B5053).

Greyhound Inn

Leek Road. Tel (01298) 84249
Grid ref: 086588
Open: 12-2.30, (closed Mon, Tue lunch) 7-11; 12-2.30, 7-10.30 Sun.

Beer: Marston's Pedigree; Black Sheep Best Bitter; Worthington Bitter.

Food: An impressive and well-priced range of up to 20 main dishes from blackboard selection. Choices may include game pie, Hartington chicken, mint and lamb casserole, spinach and red pepper lasagne, etc; plus lunchtime snacks also available. Served 12-2 (Wed-Sun only), and 7-9 each evening in either bar.

Accommodation: B&B - 2 doubles, 2 single.

General: This very welcoming 250 year old coaching inn is to be found in the centre of the village (turn off the B5053) and used to be called the Greyhound and Hare, a reference to coursing. The main room boasts an open fire at the far end and is spacious and attractively-furnished, but not cluttered, while the smaller tap room next door is more for walkers, dog-owners and where traditional bar games are held. There's live music most Saturday nights (soft rock and blues). Families welcome; small garden at rear, and outside summer seating at front.

TISSINGTON - Derbyshire

This attractive estate village, with its wide drives, exceptionally neat cottages and picture-postcard duckpond, belongs to the Fitzherbert family of Tissington Hall (recently opened to the public). Here the first Peak District well-dressing is reputed to have taken place, when in 1350 grateful villagers gave thanks to their springs that they believed had spared them from the Black Death. Today the ceremony takes place on Ascension Day, when as many as six wells are decorated with intricate floral designs.

Access: 3 miles north of Ashbourne (off A515).

Bluebell Inn

Tissington (on A515). Tel (01335) 350317
Grid ref: 172516
Open: 12-3, 5-11 (11-11 summer); 12-3, 5-10.30 (12-10.30 summer) Sun.

Beer: Bass, plus one guest such as Timothy Taylor's Landlord; Shepherd Neame Spitfire; Charles Wells Bombardier.

Food: Standard pub food (sandwiches and light snacks to full Sunday roast), served in bar or restaurant (no-smoking areas in both) throughout the day 'till 9pm (in summer), with a mid afternoon menu and teas available. Last evening orders in winter is at 8pm.

General: Located on the A515 near the Tissington Gates (the entry drive to the village) this 16th century pub remained a working farm until 1984. In its time it was a popular stop-off for coaches and drovers, and today the comfortable, refurbished interior welcomes both drivers and walkers – the Tissington Trail is only a few minutes away. Children in dining area only. Disabled access and toilets. Small beer garden with tables at side.

WETTON - Staffordshire

A small upland village and a popular base from which to explore the Manifold Valley, and in particular the dramatic Thor's Cave, high up on a rocky spur. The cave has been investigated by archaelogists who have discovered remains dating to the Stone Age.

Access: 3 ¹/₂ miles south-west of Hartington, (turn off B5054 at Hulme End).

Olde Royal Oak

Wetton. Tel (01335) 310287
Grid ref: 109554
Open 12-3, 7-11 (closed Wed winter); 12-3, 7-10.30 Sun.

Beer: Up to five, changing real ales in summer (from breweries such as Jennings, Black Sheep, Whim Hartington and Leatherbritches) and usually three in winter, plus

WARSLOW - Derbyshire

An old estate village that was re-designed in the 18th/19th centuries by the Harpur Crewe family (see entry for Crewe & Harpur Arms, West section), and which sits above the dramatic northern section of the Manifold valley.

occasional seasonal beers. Also look out for the hot mulled wine and wide range of malt whiskies.

Food: Hot and cold menu served 12-2, 7-9pm, throughout the pub (no smoking in sun lounge/family room). Daily specials board includes likes of lambs liver and onions in gravy, parsnip and leek bake, and chocolate and brandy ice cream.

Accommodation: B&B - 4 double en-suite rooms in adjacent building; family camping also available.

General: Solid, 400 year old village pub featuring two cosy bars with open fires and beamed ceilings, plus an upright piano, and newer sun lounge for families and groups. The shelves by the front door are for rucksacks and dirty boots and indicate the pub's popularity with walkers and cyclists. Beer garden and benches out the front. No dogs inside. Live music ("folky") every other Sat; and make sure not to miss the famous world toe-wrestling championships held at the pub each summer!

WHATSTANDWELL - Derbyshire

The many and various age-old crossings of the River Derwent inevitably gave rise to specific hamlets, although sometimes the origins of names have become a little muddied over time. There was certainly once a ford at this spot between Cromford and Ambergate, and according to some it was a Walter Stonewell who lived at the house on the bank and built the 14th century bridge (hence the original name of 'Wattestanwell'). There again, it could equally well come from Walter Standwell, who others claim was once a tollmaster and lived in part of the present building by the river. Take your pick.

Access: 4 miles south-east of Matlock (A6).

Derwent Hotel

Whatstandwell. Tel (01773) 856616
Grid ref: 333544
Open: 12-2.30, 7 (6 Fri)-11, 11-11 Sat;
12-10.30 Sun.

Beer: Kimberley Best Bitter, plus one Kimberley seasonal beer.

Food: Reasonably priced bar meals served 12-2.30, 6/7-9 Mon-Fri, and 12-8 at week-

ends. As well as the traditional Sunday roast, Thursday is steak night and Fridays are of course fish, but the menu also includes vegetarian options such as broccoli and cream cheese bake, and mushroom and nut fettucini.

Accommodation: B&B - 5 en-suite family and double rooms, plus 3 other rooms in main building.

General: An Inn has stood here for around 300 years and originally incorporated a toll house. The Derwent Hotel was once called the Bull's Head and served the coaches travelling the Derwent valley between Matlock and Derby. Today its bright and cheerful main room is still popular with passing travellers, as is the smart pool/darts room to the side. Children welcome in the bar 'till 9pm, plus there's an outside play area and seats to the rear. Walking groups welcome, dogs allowed inside after food serving times. Live music on the first Saturday of every month, plus occasional folk sessions on Wednesday evenings.

Homesford Cottage Inn

Derby Road/A6 (between Whatstandwell and Cromford). Tel (01629) 822342
Grid ref: 324554
Open: 12-3, 5.30-11 Mon-Thurs; 11-11 Fri, Sat, Bank and school holidays; 12-10.30 Sun.

Beer: Kimberley Best Bitter, Mild, plus a Kimberley seasonal beer.

Food: A range of light snacks (including huge filled rolls) through to hot bar food and an à la carte restaurant menu. Look out for traditional roasts, game dishes, and various pies (venison, steak and Guinness, lamb with apricot and blackcurrant, etc.) - regular fixtures are Pie and Pudding night (Thurs) and Steak and Pudding (Fridays). Served from 12 noon to 9.30pm, depending on opening times, in main bar or separate dining room (restaurant menu only). Children's menu available. No smoking in dining room and areas of main bar.

Accommodation: Riverside campsite (with facilities).

General: Originally built to serve the railway navvies who pioneered the Derwent valley line into the Peak District, this unostentatious pub is to be found on the A6 mid-way between Whatsandwell and Cromford, near High Peak Junction. There's one main bar, with open fires at either end, and a large dining room to the side. Walkers and families welcome (but no children at bar), plus in the summer there's a garden and play area to the rear.

WIRKSWORTH - Derbyshire

An attractive old town on the southern edge of the Peak District. Narrow thoroughfares and passageways (known as 'ginnels' or 'jitties') weave their way between interesting and well-preserved buildings, and reveal gems like the parish church of St Mary, with its round churchyard and carved Anglo-Saxon coffin lid. Wirksworth is closely associated with the novelist George Eliot, and appears as 'Snowfield' in her novel Adam Bede. For more information visit Wirksworth Heritage Centre above Crown Yard (off the market place).

Access: 4 miles south of Matlock (B5036).

Black's Head

Market Place. Tel (01629) 823257
Grid ref: 286539
Open: 11.30-3, 6-11; 11-11 Sat;
12-4, 7-10.30 Sun.
Beer: Kimberley Best Bitter, Classic.
Food: Served lunchtimes only (12-2). Wide choice of delicious home made soup which may feature Thai chicken noodle, butternut squash and Italian bean and vegetable. Highly recommended. Although on the soups blackboard the 'chunky chick, veg and two yorks' and the Highlander's broth are in fact substantial and good value main meals. A range of filled baguettes (such as asparagus and brie) are also available.
General: Handsome one room, brick built pub overlooking the market place, originally called the Blackamoors Head. Comfortable and relaxed atmosphere, usually with piped jazz music in the background. No children under 14; dogs allowed outside food serving times.

> *The Peak District has over 22 million visitors each year, but the resident population is only about 38,000*

WIRKSWORTH MOOR - Derbyshire

Hilltop location a mile to the east of Wirksworth (on B5035).

Malt Shovel Inn

Wirksworth Moor. Tel (01629) 822427
Grid ref: 299541
Open: 11-11; 12-10.30 Sun.
Beer: Marston's Pedigree.
Food: Bar snacks served lunchtimes only (12-2.30), such as sandwiches, toasties, etc.
General: Solid and pleasant roadside pub dating from the late 19th/early 20th century. Below the small and open main bar is a pool room, suitable for children, while outside there's a large floodlit boules pitch across the road by the car park (which used to be the tennis court belonging to the original building), and a small area of children's swings and tables to the side. Dogs allowed inside, and walkers are welcome to eat their own food on the premises.

> *"When you have lost your inns,*
> *Drown your empty selves*
> *For you will have lost the last of England."*
> Hillaire Belloc

A - L Index by pub name

Anchor Inn, Tideswell (C/E) 34
Anglers Rest, Bamford (N)41
Angler's Rest, Miller's Dale (C/E) 26
Ashford Arms, Ashford in the Water (C/E) 11
Bakers Arms, Buxton (W) 68
Barley Mow, Bonsall (C/E) 16
Barley Mow, Kirk Ireton (S) 94
Barrel Inn, Bretton (N) 44
Bear Inn, Alderwasley (S) 83
Beehive, Combs (W) 72
Beehive, New Mills (W) 76
Bell Inn, Cromford (S) 89
Bentley Brook Inn, Fenny Bentley (S) 89
Black Lion Inn, Butterton (S) 87
Black Swan, Ashover (C/E) 11
Black Swan, Crich (S) 88
Black's Head, Wirksworth (S) 99
Bluebell Inn, Tissington (S) 97
Boat House, Matlock (C/E) 23
Boat Inn, Cromford (S) 89
Bowling Green, Ashbourne (S) 84
Bridge Inn, Calver (N) 44
Bull i' th' Thorn, Hurdlow (C/E) 22
Bull's Head, Ashford in the Water (C/E) 11
Bull's Head, Castleton (N) 45
Bull's Head, Foolow (N) 48
Bull's Head, Glossop (N) 49
Bull's Head, Monyash (C/E) 28
Bull's Head, Youlgrave (C/E) 37
Castle Hotel, Castleton (N) 45
Castle Inn, Bakewell (C/E) 12
Cat and Fiddle, Cat and Fiddle (W) 70
Cavalier, Grindon (S) 90
Charles Cotton Hotel, Hartington (S) 91
Chequers Inn, Froggatt Edge (N) 49
Cheshire Cheese Inn, Hope (N) 55
Church House Inn, Bollington (W) 65
Church Inn, Chelmorton (C/E) 17
Church Inn, Darley Dale (C/E) 18
Cliff Inn, Crich (S) 88
Coach and Horses, Fenny Bentley (S) 90
Cock and Pullet, Sheldon (C/E) 31
Crag Inn, Wildboarclough (W) 79
Crewe and Harpur Arms, Longnor (W) 75
Crispin, Ashover (C/E) 12
Crispin Inn, Great Longstone (C/E) 21
Crown, Matlock (C/E) 24
Dandy Cock, Disley (W) 72
Derwent Hotel, Bamford (N) 41
Derwent Hotel, Whatstandwell (S) 98
Derwentwater Arms, Calver (N) 44
Devonshire Arms, Baslow (C/E) 14

Devonshire Arms, Beeley (C/E) 15
Devonshire Arms, Hartington (S) 91
Devonshire Arms, Peak Forest (N) 60
Devonshire Arms, Pilsley (C/E) 29
Diggle Hotel, Diggle (N) 46
Druid Inn, Birchover (C/E) 16
Duke of Wellington, Matlock (C/E) 24
Duke of York, Elton (C/E) 20
Duke of York, Pomeroy (C/E) 29
Duke William, Matlock (C/E) 25
Eyre Arms, Hassop (C/E) 21
Farmyard Inn, Youlgrave (C/E) 37
Fishpond, Matlock Bath (C/E) 26
Fleece Inn, Holme (N) 54
Fox House, Longshaw (N) 58
Friendship Inn, Glossop (N) 50
Flying Childers, Stanton in Peak (C/E) 32
George, Alstonefield (S) 83
George Hotel, Castleton (N) 45
George Hotel, Hayfield (N) 53
George Hotel, Tideswell (C/E) 34
George Hotel, Youlgrave (C/E) 37
Goyt Inn, Whaley Bridge (W) 78
Great Western, Marsden (N) 58
Green Man Royal Hotel, Ashbourne (S) 84
Greyhound Inn, Warslow (S) 97
Grouse Inn, Darley Dale (C/E) 18
Grouse Inn, Longshaw (N) 58
Grouse and Claret, Rowsley (C/E) 30
Hanging Gate, Chapel-en-le-Frith (W) 70
Hanging Gate, Langley (W) 74
Highwayman, Eastmoor (C/E) 20
Highwayman, Rainow (W) 77
Hollybush Inn, Grangemill (C/E) 21
Homesford Cottage Inn - Whatstandwell (S) 98
Horse and Jockey, Tideswell (C/E) 34
Horseshoe Inn, Longnor (W) 75
Izaak Walton Hotel, Ilam (S) 93
Jervis Arms, Onecote (W) 77
Jovial Dutchman, Crich (S) 88
Jug and Glass, Newhaven (C/E) 28
Jug and Glass, Lea (S) 95
King's Arms Hotel, Chapel-en-le-Frith (W) 71
King's Head, Bonsall (C/E) 17
Knockerdown Inn, Knockerdown (S) 94
Ladybower Inn, Ladybower Reservoir (N) 56
Lamb Inn, Chinley Head (W) 71
Lantern Pike Inn, Little Hayfield (N) 57
Lathkil Hotel, Over Haddon (C/E) 29
Lazy Trout, Meerbrook (W) 76
Leathers Smithy, Langley (W) 74
Little John Hotel, Hathersage (N) 52

100

Appendices

1: Pubs with regular live music

CENTRAL/EAST
Bakewell: **Wheatsheaf** (Sat eve, bands)
Darley Dale: **Grouse Inn** (Sat eve, jazz monthly)
Earl Sterndale: **Quiet Woman** (most Sundays, folk, C&W)
Little Longstone: **Packhorse Inn** (Wed eve, folk sessions)
Litton: **Red Lion** (occasional jazz and folk sessions)
Monyash: **Bull's Head** (fortnightly Sat, singing/vocals)
Pilsley: **Devonshire Arms** (fortnightly Wed, 60s, C&W)
Tideswell: **George Hotel** (Fri eve, 60s/70s)
Wardlow Mires: **Three Stags Heads** (Sat eve, folk sessions)

NORTH
Bretton: **Barrel Inn** (Wed eve, Irish folk sessions)
Castleton: **Bull's Head** and **Olde Cheshire Cheese** (both monthly folk sessions)
Foolow: **Bull's Head** (pianist Fri and Sun lunchtimes)
Grindleford: **Sir William Hotel** (Sun, 60s/70s)
Hathersage: **Millstone Inn** (bands last Fri in month), **Scotsman's Pack** (jazz first Mon in month)
Hayfield: **George Hotel** (jazz, Sun afternoons)
Rowarth: **Little Mill Inn** (Fri eve, local bands)

SOUTH
Bonsall: **Barley Mow** (Sat eve and sessions)
Matlock Bath: **Fishpond** (twice weekly gigs and Sun session)
Crich: **Black Swan** (monthly guitar/duo)
Kniveton: **Red Lion** (monthly folk sessions)
Lea: **Jug & Glass** (Sun, folk)
Middleton-by-Wirksworth: **Rising Sun** (Fri/Sat live acts)
Warslow: **Greyhound Inn** (Sat eve, soft rock/blues)
Wetton: **Olde Royal Oak** (Sat fortnightly, folk)
Whatstandwell: **Derwent Hotel** (live act first Sat in month)

WEST
Bottom-of-the-Oven: **Stanley Arms** (singer every third Fri of month)
Buxton: **Bakers Arms** (Sun eve, Irish duo)
Chapel-en-le-Frith: **King's Arms Hotel** (bands weekly) **Roebuck Inn** (singer one Sat eve per month)
Flash Bar: **Traveller's Rest** (jazz first Thurs of month)
Longnor: **Horseshoe Inn** (Fri eve, folk, blues, C&W)

2: Pubs offering campsite, camping barn or caravan facilities

CENTRAL/EAST
Darley Bridge: **Square and Compass**
Darley Dale: **Plough**
Earl Sterndale: **Quiet Woman**
Hurdlow: **Bull i' th' Thorn**, **Royal Oak**
Matlock: **Duke William**
Rowsley: **Grouse and Claret**

Winster: **Miner's Standard**
NORTH
Castleton: **Bull's Head**
Snake Pass: **Snake Pass Inn**
SOUTH
Alstonefield: **George**
Biggin: **Waterloo Inn**
Knockerdown: **Knockerdown Inn**
Wetton: **Olde Royal Oak**
Whatstandwell: **Homesford Cottage Inn**
WEST
Longnor: **Crewe and Harpur Arms**

3: Pubs which normally serve food after 9.30pm (recommend you ring ahead to check)

CENTRAL/EAST
Eastmoor: **Highwayman**
Grangemill: **Hollybush Inn**
Matlock: **Crown**
NORTH
Birch Vale: **Sycamore Inn**
Castleton: **Castle Inn**
Glossop: **Bull's Head, Nag's Head**
Hathersage: **Little John Hotel**
Longshaw: **Fox House**
Rowarth: **Little Mill Inn**
SOUTH
Biggin: **Waterloo Inn**
Hartington: **Charles Cotton Hotel**
WEST
Bollington: **Poachers Inn**
Buxton: **Wye Bridge House**
Chapel-en-le-Frith: **Hanging Gate, Royal Oak**
Disley: **Ram's Head**
Langley: **Leathers Smithy**
New Mills: **Pack Horse Inn**
Onecote: **Jervis Arms**

4: Pubs with a great view

CENTRAL/EAST
Matlock: **Thorn Tree Inn**
Monsal Head: **Stables Bar (Monsal Head Hotel)**
Over Haddon: **Lathkil Hotel**
NORTH
Bradfield: **Old Horns Inn**
Bretton: **Barrel Inn**
Hathersage: **Millstone Inn**
Strines: **Strines Inn**
SOUTH
Alderwasley: **Bear Inn**
Dovedale: **Izaak Walton Hotel**
WEST
Cat and Fiddle: **Cat and Fiddle Inn**
Langley: **Hanging Gate**
New Mills: **Packhorse Inn**
Strines: **Sportsman's Arms**
Thorncliffe: **Mermaid Inn**